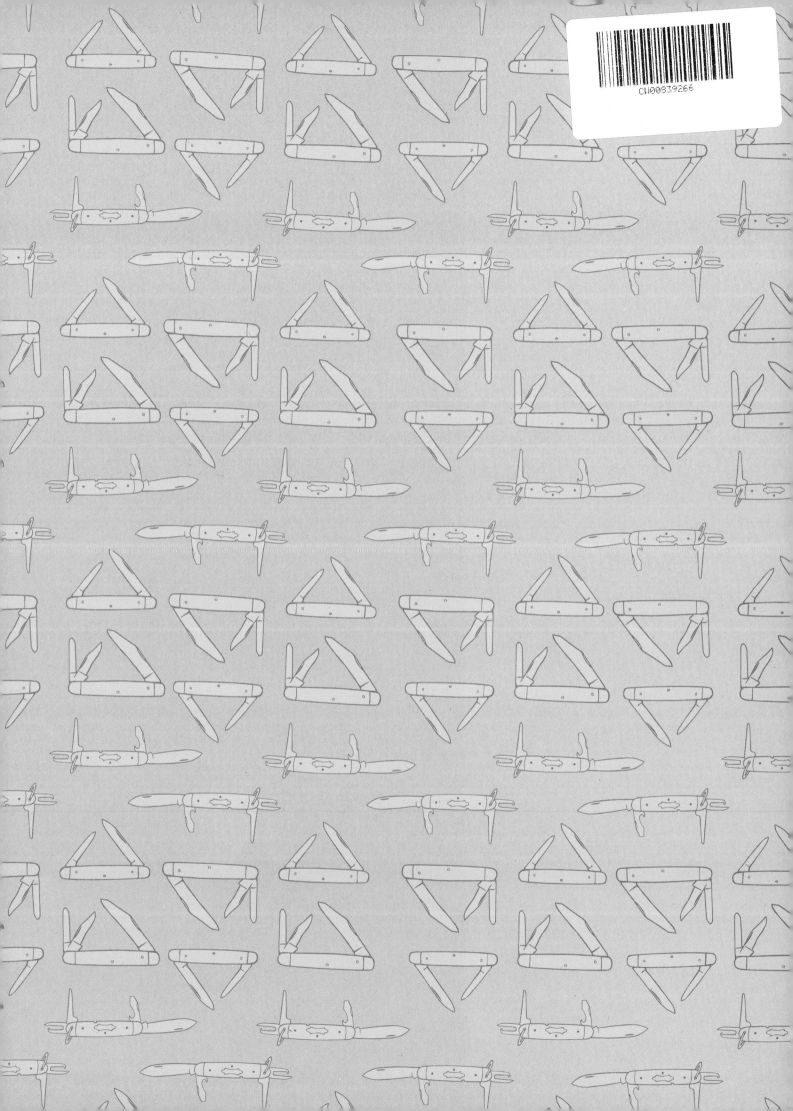

# POCKET-KNIVES

# POCKET-KNIVES

## THE COLLECTOR'S GUIDE TO IDENTIFYING, BUYING AND ENJOYING VINTAGE POCKETKNIVES

**Bernard Levine**

THE
APPLE
PRESS

A QUINTET BOOK

Published by The Apple Press
6 Blundell Street
London, N7 9BH

ISBN 1–85076–425–5

This book was designed and produced by
Quintet Publishing Limited
6 Blundell Street
London N7 9BH

**Creative Director:** Richard Dewing
**Project Editor:** Katie Preston
**Editor:** Maggi McCormick
**Photographer:** Harry Rinker Jr.
**Designer:** Peter Laws

Typeset in Great Britain by
Central Southern Typesetters, Eastbourne
Manufactured in Singapore by Eray Scan Pte Limted
Printed in Hong Kong by
Leefung-Asco Printers Limited

**Acknowledgement**
The chapter "Hand Crafted Folding Knives" is a
revised and updated version of the author's article,
"Whither Hand-Made Folders – and Why," in the
*Blade Magazine Special Issue: Custom Knives*,
Summer 1989. Used by permission.


We would like to thank the following for their help with the photographs in this book:

The members of the Mason-Dixon Knife Club ● Simon
Moore ● Barett-Smythe Limited ● The Forschner Group ●
Dr H. Melnick ● Victorinox Cutlery Limited ● Jim Hughes
● Remington ● Imperial Schrade Corporation ● Bernard
Levine ● Weyer International of Toledo ● National Knife
Collectors Association ● Robert Wentz ● The American
Military Edged Weaponry Museum

The circa 1910 drawings in the chapter "Making
Pocketknives" where previously reproduced in *The Romance
of Knife Collecting, 4th Ed.* by Mrs L. Ferguson, published
in 1976 and long out of print. They were also reproduced in
*Knife World* magazine. Used by permission.

# CONTENTS

# INTRODUCTION

Pocketknives. At first glance they seem such an everyday item, one might wonder why so many people collect them. Yet it is precisely the familiar charm and infinite variety of the commonplace that gives them their appeal. After all, what could be more familiar than coins and postage stamps, the most popular collector items of all?

Coins and pocketknives share a place in a pocket or handbag, yet our attachment to coins is fleeting. We spend them, we drop them into fountains, we give them to children. A pocketknife, by contrast, once we have found a satisfactory one, is a companion for years, even for life. We are the tool-using creatures *par excellence*, and the one tool we are always sure to have with us is a pocketknife.

And a pocketknife is more than merely a tool. It is also a mechanical device, sometimes a very complex one. It is a work of craft and technology, certainly, but it can be equally a work of art.

To the affluent and sophisticated, fine pocketknives are personal jewellery. They have been so for centuries, much as they are today. In 1862 President Abraham Lincoln was

ABOVE
**Case XX Made in USA 5-dot (1975) premium pen knife, red bone handles**

presented with a handsome five-blade knife, a knife that recently sold at auction for nearly $100,000 (£60,000). Today exclusive shops, such as the world-famous Barrett-Smythe Galleries in New York City; Hawthorn Galleries in Branson, Missouri; the S.F. Gun Exchange in San Francisco; OK-YESS Knives in Tokyo; Yamanaka Knife Shop in Osaka; World Knives Gallery in Yokohama; Messer Hessel in Braunschweig, Germany; Messer Klötzli in Burgdorf, Switzerland; G. Lorenzi in Milan; E. Lorenzi in Vienna; and M. Kindal in Paris, sell exquisite contemporary hand-crafted folding knives, some of them engraved by the world's leading engravers, at prices that range from several hundred dollars up to $50,000 (£30,000) each.

Beyond these technical, aesthetic, and status considerations, a pocketknife of any age (even a brand-new one) is an historical artifact that was made in a particular time and place, by particular people, and for a particular market. With study and experience one can learn to read these artifacts as precisely as an archaeologist reads potsherds.

Because the pocketknife is universal, and because its history is ancient, its forms, its varieties, and its brands have multiplied beyond imagining. Efforts to document and classify them approach in complexity the work of paleontologists on the taxonomy of fossils. Less than half of the five thousand or so observed pocketknife brands have been documented, and old brands are rediscovered every day. Most of those brands represented between two dozen and two thousand distinct patterns – even more if the brand spanned several generations, or if it was distributed worldwide.

Yet despite this dizzying complexity, the broad framework of the pocketknife story – people, cities, nations, companies, technology, design – has been elucidated in recent years. Two decades ago, books that even touched on the subject numbered fewer than ten. Today there are many dozens of knife books, along with periodicals by the score (see the critical bibliography at the end of this book). The dedicated research of hundreds of collectors and historians is gathered in those thousands of pages, and the essence of their years of work has been distilled into the volume you now hold.

In this book, for the first time, the broad and factual story of pocketknives, mainly in the past century and a half, is presented

ABOVE
**"The Primate Knife."**
**Folding knife by Ron Lake,**
**3½ in (8.75cm) long closed,**
**with gold engraved eyeglass**
**screwdriver in the handle.**
**Inlaid with gold and**
**engraved by Ron Smith.**

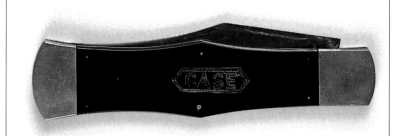

RIGHT
**Large Case store display knife 11¼ in (28.6cm) long closed, slick black composition handles.**

ABOVE
**German style folding bowie, "Le Louis d'Or" (gold coin brand) made in France, stag handles.**

ABOVE
**Empire Knife Co, West Winsted, Conn, silver handled figural knife.**

in one narrative, as one coherent picture. It is presented from the viewpoint of the collector or knife fancier, explaining why certain knives are interesting, collectible, and – in consequence – valuable.

This book is a basic introduction, and as such assumes no foreknowledge about knives on the part of the reader. Nonetheless, there is a wealth of information here that will prove valuable and revealing to the most advanced collector or knife dealer, and even to manufacturers who have spent a lifetime in the cutlery industry.

Pocketknife collecting is more developed as a hobby in the US than elsewhere – although interest has grown remarkably in recent years in Canada, Britain, Australia, France, Germany, Austria, Italy, Switzerland, and Japan. Pocketknives made for the American market are the primary focus of collectors today, although as the hobby advances, collectors everywhere will, I am sure, explore the history of their own indigenous pocketknife traditions more thoroughly.

# CHAPTER
# I

# HISTORY OF
# POCKETKNIVES

The pocketknife is such a familiar item that it has largely been invisible to the historian. Picture the diligent chronicler, carefully sharpening his quill pen with his pen knife before setting down the record of glorious deeds, and it is easy to understand his overlooking the seemingly mundane story of that sharp little knife.

In consequence the story of pocketknives prior to the 18th century is part conjectural, part archaeological. Excavations have revealed charming figural folding knives that evidently date from the later years of the Roman Empire – which means that they were not "pocketknives", since sewn-on pockets had not yet been invented. Like early scientific and navigation instruments, ancient and medieval folding knives made up for their technical deficiencies with an abundance of exuberant decoration.

Those earliest-known folding knives had no backsprings in their handles. The job of a pocketknife's spring is to apply tension to the blade, to keep it in place both open and closed. Without a spring, friction alone must be relied upon to keep a folding blade from flopping about.

To this day inexpensive folding knives are made in the Ancient

ABOVE
**Roman folding knife, the bronze openwork haft cast in the form of a hound catching a rabbit. 2nd–4th century AD.**

ABOVE
**Roman folding knife handle (base missing) depicting an embracing couple in bronze. The way her robe is slipping off suggests a Gallo-Roman design 3rd–4th century AD.**

BELOW
**Medieval folding knife with Gothic style brass handle, c1400.**

Roman style, without backsprings, by cutlers in France, Spain, Japan, and China. One popular name for these is "penny knives", because until recent years the plainest versions of such knives sold for a penny apiece.

Although the idea of the spring-back knife seems to be older, reliable spring steel was a product of the mid-18th century – 1742 to be precise. It was the invention of a clock maker in Sheffield, England, called Benjamin Huntsman. Sheffield's cutlers soon learned to use Huntsman's crucible cast steel for both the blades and the springs of their finer cutlery items, and on this new metal, more than anything else, was the city's world pre-eminence as a cutlery center based.

The generation after Huntsman's invention witnessed remarkable advances in cutlery design and technology, nowhere more than in Paris, France. Much of the basic design and technology of modern cutlery was created there at that time, largely by one man, master cutler Jean-Jacques Perret. Perret thoughtfully set down a detailed and thoroughly illustrated record of his work in three folio volumes, *The Art of the Cutler*, published in 1771, and also in his autobiography. More than a century later, "inventors" in America, Britain, and Germany were still regularly receiving patents for cutlery mechanisms copied line for line from Perret's books.

Factory mass-production of cheap pocketknives – penny knives – also dates from 18th-century France – a detailed account
was published in 1771. Yet from then into the middle of the 19th century, better grades of folding knives were made one at a time by highly skilled craftsmen, primarily in England, France, Germany, Italy, and Bohemia.

Because high-quality folding knives were then made by hand, the variety of patterns and styles of pocketknives offered in the early 19th century was seemingly endless. However, as widely dispersed mass markets began to develop, especially in the western hemisphere, standardization of pocketknife patterns for sale in those markets gradually advanced.

Perhaps the most remarkable folding knives in that period of great diversity (especially in the view of today's collectors) were the folding sidearms. Ornate and often very large folding dirks, folding bowie knives, and folding knife-pistol combinations were made in almost endless variation in Sheffield, both for sale at home and for export to America, from the 1830s into the early part of the 20th century. Almost as great a variety of folding sidearms, up to the size of folding cutlasses, was produced in Western Europe, including France, Belgium, Germany, Austria, Italy, and Spain. Rim-fire pocketknife-pistols in .22 calibre were made in the US in the 1920s and 1930s, while German firms offered gun-dog training knife-pistols which employed pinfire blanks.

Beginning in the 1840s, emigrant cutlers from Europe began to develop a pocket cutlery industry in the United States. In America, where land and resources were plentiful, but skilled labour was scarce, cutlery manufacturers pioneered machine methods and simplified processes – another force favouring standardized patterns. Innovative men like Samuel Mason and C. W. Platts of Northfield Knife Co, Homer Twitchell of Waterville Mfg Co, Matthew Chapman of J. Russell & Co, and Joseph Gardner of Lamson & Goodnow, most of them Sheffield-trained prior to 1860, laid down the technological foundations of the burgeoning American cutlery industry. Meanwhile, traditional hand methods remained near-universal in Sheffield through the 1890s, and still exist there, on a very limited scale.

The story of a pocketknife can often be read on the *tangs* of its blades – the tang is a blade's unsharpened extension, which is fixed into the handle. Blade tangs are usually stamped with the name or trademark of the firm which distributed the knife. This firm might be the actual manufacturer, or alternatively an importer, wholesaler, or retailer.

The evolution of pocketknives from the 1880s up to 1940 is primarily a story of marketing, design, and above all tariffs. Technology was remarkably stable in that period, viewed by collectors today as the "Golden Age" of pocket cutlery. The most important cutlery innovation of that period, the invention of stainless steel in 1914 (simultaneously by Sheffield metallurgist Harry Brearley and Indiana chemist Elwood Haynes), revolutionized table cutlery, but it had little or no affect on the pocket cutlery industry until after 1950. The story of that Golden Age, and of the Dark Age and Renaissance of pocket cutlery which followed, is recounted in detail in the chapters which follow.

**ABOVE**
**A. G. Alford Sporting Goods, Baltimore, Md (late 19th-century retailer), large horseman's knife, made in Sheffield, genuine stag handles. Note thumb lancet, pick, and tweezers concealed in handle; 6 in (15.25cm) long closed.**

# JACK KNIFE, PEN KNIFE AND MULTI-BLADE

TOP
**Ka-Bar limited edition
lockback English jack with
folding guard, bone stag
handles, dog-head shield.**
—

BOTTOM
**James Ward & Co,
Bronxville, NY, rare
American made folding dirk
with folding guard, horn
handles, c1860s.**

All pocketknives can be divided into three basic types, on the basis of structure. Functionally, by contrast, there are dozens of different types of folding knife. The three structural types are jack knives, pen knives, and multi-blades.

Like the taxonomy of plants and animals, the taxonomy of pocketknives has its share of ambiguity, fuzzy boundaries, and polite disagreement among experts. Still, all folding knives can reasonably be assigned to one of these three types.

········· JACK KNIVES AND PEN KNIVES ·········

"Jack knives" are stout and simply made. As a rule a jack knife has its blade or blades (often two, very rarely three) in one end of the handle.

"Pen knives", as a rule, are delicate and finely made. They have their blades – generally two to four, occasionally more – in both ends. Some pen knives include a nail-file manicure blade.

Just to make life interesting, there are exceptions to both of these rules. Stout knives with a large blade in each end are called "double-end jack knives". Very small knives with a single tiny blade in one end are the original "pen knives", designed for

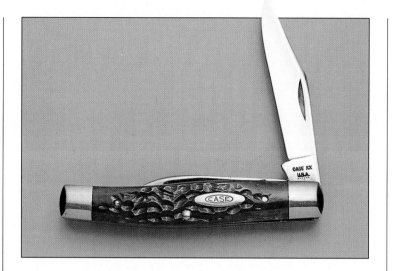

LEFT
**Case XX USA 6-dot (1974)
premium jack, red jigged
bone handles.**

sharpening quill pens. To avoid confusion collectors now call
these "quill knives".

**WHITTLERS** In addition to ordinary pen knives and quill
knives, the "pen knife" designation also embraces two distinctive
sub-types. These are called "whittlers" (a modern collector
name) and "lobsters" (a traditional cutlery industry name).

A basic whittler is a three-blade knife. It has two backsprings
which are separated at one end, but which abut each other at the
other end. At the end where the two springs touch, there is
mounted a stout master blade as thick as both springs together.
At the opposite end are mounted two shorter and thinner blades,
one on each of the springs.

This particular combination of blades makes larger "whittlers"
well suited for whittling. However, the same construction was
also used on smaller, more delicate three-blade pen knives,
which collectors also call "whittlers".

Most pocketknife manufacture has been substantially
automated today, even the process of making simple lobster
pen knives (such as the Victorinox Classic). However, whittler
construction still requires a lot of skilled hand-work, and the
pattern is now virtually extinct, except for a few hand-makers or
as costly German-made limited editions.

The earliest whittler-type knives, made in 18th-century Paris,
had a single spring split down the middle for most of its length.
Using two springs proved both easier and stronger. In some
whittlers a tapered centre liner divides the two springs for most of

TOP
**Ka-Bar limited edition
jumbo whittler, genuine
stag, serial #111.**

BOTTOM
**Cattaraugus Cutlery Co,
Little Valley, NY, sunfish,
bone stag handles.**

ABOVE
**Case Tested double-end
premium jack, "rough-
black" composition handles.**

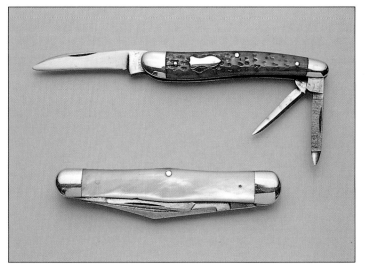

## JACKKNIVES

**Notes:**

(FH = large version used as folding hunter die)
(DE = also used as double-end jack knife die)
• Equal-End Jack (DE) *Sunfish (Elephant Toenail) (DE only)* • Slim Equal-End Jack
• Regular Jack *Electrician's Knife, Barlow Knife, Boy's Knife, No 2 Scout Knife, English Jack (FH), Stabber pattern* • Slim Jack (Slim Regular Jack) *Melon Tester, Physician's Knife* • Curved Regular Jack (FH) *Rope Knife* • Sleeveboard Jack *US WWI Electrician's Knife* • Jumbo Jack (large Sleeveboard) (DE) • Curved Jack (as on the traditional British farmer's knife) *Pruning Knife, Maize (grain sorghum) Knife, Cotton Sampler, Rope Knife, Whaler* • Swayback Jack
• Congress Jack • Crown Jack (also called Coffin Jack) • Swell-End Jack ("Tear Drop") • Swell-Centre Jack ("Coke Bottle") (FH)
• Balloon Jack (DE) *Platts Sunfish (DE Only)* • Swell-Centre Regular Jack (FH) *Trapper, Large Trapper* • Gunstock Jack *Gunstock Budding Knife* • Premium Jack (DE) *Premium Trapper (DE)* •Gunstock Premium Jack • Serpentine Jack *Peanut, Wharncliffe Jack (DE)* • Slim Serpentine Jack *Light Trapper* • Eureka Jack (Swell-Centre Serpentine Balloon Jack) (DE)
• Canoe (DE) • Surveyor (Swell-Centre Canoe) (DE) • Fishtail Jack • Fish Jack
• Tickler (Powder Horn) *Fish Knife* • Clasp type (FH only)

their length. In others, a stubby "catch bit" divides only the two small blades from each other. A knife with *three* blades and *three* springs is not a whittler.

A few highly skilled Sheffield cutlers (some of whom emigrated to the US) made five-blade whittlers: one large blade, four small blades, three springs. These are rare, elegant, and valuable.

**LOBSTERS** A "lobster" is a pen knife with blades at both top and bottom, and with its springs therefore concealed inside the centre of the handle. Lobsters are fragile and elegant. Before World War II, they were among the most costly of pocketknives, but today most collectors prefer larger knives which make a more impressive display.

ABOVE
**Case XX USA 1971
"Hawbaker's Special"
improved muskrat, red bone
stag handles.**

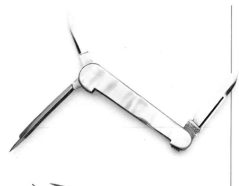

TOP
**W.R. Case & Sons "opal
pearl" Sheffield-pattern
lobster.**

BOTTOM
**Victorinox "Classic" equal-
end lobster penknife.**

RIGHT
**Miller Bros Cutlery,
Meriden, Conn, swell-centre
hunting knife, ebony. The
use of tiny screws to retain
the handles was a
registered
trademark of
Miller Bros.**

**FOLDING HUNTERS**  Today's knife collectors favour big
folding knives, especially the folding hunting knives. Folding
hunters are generally 4½ to 5½ inches (11 to 14 cm) long when
closed. They have one or two large blades and are a type of
jack knife.

Classic folding hunters were made on a variety of standard
handle dies (see page 18): the swell-centre or "Coke bottle", the
swell-centre regular or "Trapper style", and four or five variations
on the curved clasp knife. Many firms still make clasp-type
folding hunters, but their popularity has declined substantially
since the 1960s.

Virtually all modern-style folding hunters, with their curved
grip and stout metal frame, were either copied or derived from a
single innovative prototype – the original Buck Model 110 folding
hunter, introduced in 1962. Buck now makes many variations on

## LOBSTER PENKNIVES
· · · · · · · · · · · · · · · · · ·

**Note:** (LWH = also made as lobster whittlers)

Oval Lobster (Charm Knife) ● Equal-End Lobster ● Sunfish Lobster ● Dolphin (Fish Candle-End Lobster) ● Sleeveboard Lobster (LWH) ● Sheffield Pattern Lobster ● Serpentine Lobster ● Serpentine Candle-End Lobster ● Gunstock Lobster *Orange Blossom* (LWH)

TOP
**Case XX Made in USA 4-dot (1976) premium stock knife, red jigged bone handles.**

BOTTOM
**Case USA (1980) prototype gunboat (three-blade canoe cattle knife), genuine stag handles.**

BELOW
**Victorinox "Swiss Champ," currently the firm's largest model multi-blade.**

its original design, and the 110 itself has seen quite an evolution of form and technology. Today there is hardly a single pocketknife factory or hand-craftsman of folding knives who does not make knives that are based at least in part on Buck's revolutionary 1962 design.

· · · · · · · · · · · · · · · · · · MULTI-BLADES · · · · · · · · · · · · · · · · · ·

The category "multi-blade" includes all knives with three or more blades, of which one or more are gadget-type blades such as bottle- or tin-openers, leather punches, corkscrews, forks, and spoons.

The multi-blade category also usually includes stout knives with three or more cutting blades, one or more of which is a special-purpose blade. Mainly these are "cattle knives" and "premium stock knives".

Cattle-knife handle dies have names, because most of them are built on the same frames as double-end jack knives. Other multi-blade shapes are not named, but are grouped into broad categories, such as scout-utility knives, horseman's knives, sportsman's knives, cattle knives, stock knives, plier and wrench knives (including miner's dynamite knives), and knife-fork-spoon combinations. Unusual gadget-type multi-blades are shown in Chapter 3.

LEFT
**Kutmaster, 3⅜ in. (8.5cm) green plastic handles with hot stamp shield, four blades.**

ABOVE
**Case XX M4045 utility knife with metal handles, British-style tin-opener blade.**

**SCOUT KNIVES AND SOLDIER KNIVES** Perhaps the most familiar American multi-blade is the scout-utility knife. The American version has four blades (rarely three, five, or six), in the same equal-end handle as the standard cattle knife, which was one of the scout-utility's two parents, the other being the European sportsman's knife. In this pattern, there have been more than thirty different Official Boy Scout knives, more than a dozen Official Girl Scout knives, and at least five Official Campfire knives. Commercial versions number in the hundreds.

American Boy Scouts, Girl Scouts, Campfire Girls, and ordinary consumers have used millions of these knives since their introduction *circa* 1910. American soldiers and marines have used countless millions more since the US armed forces adopted this pattern in 1941.

British and Commonwealth scout and military folding knives have a different lineage; they were derived from the stout sailor's jack knives of the 18th century (or perhaps earlier). In a sort of convergent evolution, they have come to embody many of the same features as their American counterparts.

US sailors used British-style sailor's jack knives until World War I, when a smaller, American version was adopted. In World War II the American Navy switched to fixed bladed knives, except for medical staff (who used utility knives) and lifeboat stores (which included folding rope knives).

Allied special operations units in World War II commissioned a wide variety of knives for secret missions from both American and British cutlery firms. Most were unmarked and had fixed blades, but some were folding knives. One distinctive type was

ABOVE
**Camillus easy-open regular jack with jigged bone handles and steel mounts, made for the US Army in World War II.**

BELOW
**Imperial five blade official Boy Scout (USA) knife, Delrin plastic handles.**

an all-metal pliers-type multi-blade, similar to a miner's dynamite knife, but incorporating a tin-opener and three hacksaw blades.

**SPORTSMAN'S KNIVES** Sportsman's knives are elaborate multi-blades with a multitude of specialized blades. Today's most familiar sportsman's knives are the "Swiss Army" knives made both by Elsener/Victorinox of Ibach and by Wenger of Delemont – and imitated by scores of firms worldwide. Today, "Swiss Army" knives are made in dozens of different models, but in earlier times there was vastly more variety in this type of knife – in size, in shape, in blade types, and in sheer complexity. Some late 18th- and early 19th-century horseman's knives (the name for sportsman's knives with a folding hoof-pick on the back) even had blades folding up inside other blades.

Today red plastic is the usual handle material on this type of knife. In the old days, genuine stag was standard, but metal, bone, horn, ivory, tortoise-shell, and pearl were options – and most of these handle materials are still available on special order on Swiss-made knives.

## ··· HANDLE DIES AND NAMED PATTERNS····

The sheet metal frame pieces (called "liners") of a pocketknife handle were stamped with a set of steel dies, and each different shape came to be called a "handle die". Every jack knife and pen knife handle die has a name, some of them unusual or attractive. The names we use today are the result of a standardization of patterns that developed between about 1840

ABOVE
**W. R. Case & Sons small rope knife with manicure blade, made for the US Navy in World War I, Rogers Mfg Co jigged bone handles.**

RIGHT
**Unmarked Central European horseman's combination knife, genuine stag handles. Blades: clip master blade, pen blade, combination saw/tin-opener, scissors, hoof-pick with attached carriage key, hollow leather punch, corkscrew.**

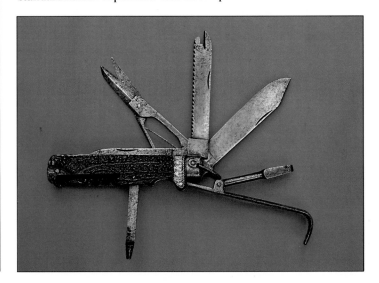

and 1890. The great multitude of now-extinct handle dies offered before that period probably had names as well, but most of them seem to have been lost.

"Handle die" refers to the shape of a pocketknife's handle. "Pattern" is even more specific, indicating a particular combination of handle-die and blades. In a cutlery catalogue, the term "pattern" is even more precise; a particular pattern number specifies handle die, size, blades, mount materials, and handle material.

The standard handle-die names of the period circa 1865–1965 are listed on pages 14 and 15. After each handle-die name are named patterns built on these dies. Some are no longer made, while most of the modern shapes introduced since that time have not yet been given names.

## BRITISH POCKETKNIFE PATTERNS

While much of Sheffield's output went to American and colonial markets, the city's most important single cutlery market was Britain itself, especially after 1891. Every pocketknife firm in Sheffield made a selection of "town patterns", pocketknife patterns typical of Sheffield, and sold in the home market.

Best known of the town patterns was the horseman's multi-blade. At its most basic, this pattern includes a spear blade, pen blade, and saw on top, with a corkscrew, augur, punch, and combined hoof-pick-nut-cracker on the bottom. Other town patterns included the senator and congress pen knives (developed originally for the American trade), the sailor's knife

**BELOW**
**Digby's, Kelham Island (Sheffield), contemporary de luxe presentation knife, pearl, engraving, filework.**

**LEFT**
**H. G. Long & Co, Sheffield, sportsman's combination knife with genuine stag handles. Blades: patent adjustable shotshell extractor, spear master blade, large buttoner for gaiters, corkscrew.**

TOP
**German Pirate logo combination knife, green horn handles. Blades: spear master blade, small screwdriver/cap-lifter, lobster manicure blade, magnifier.**

BOTTOM
**R. J. Richter, Germany, angler's pliers knife, dark red composition handles with inset hook hone. Blades: clip master blade, fish-scaler/hook-disgorger/crown cap-lifter, Phillips screwdriver, pliers with split-shot crimper, tweezers in handle.**

used by the military, the "church window", and the curved jack knife with sheepfoot blade favoured by farmers from the Channel Islands to the Orkneys, and from Dover to Donegal.

The English version of the folding hunting knife (so typical that Americans called it the "English jack") was a simple regular or sleeveboard pattern, 4 to 7 inches (10 to 17 cm) long when closed, with a single locking clip or spear point blade. The favourite lobster pattern in Britain (called the "Sheffield pattern lobster" by Americans) was a bolstered sleeveboard with an extra-wide manicure blade let into the back. As late as 1970, Wostenholm's was making large quantities of Sheffield pattern lobsters to be sold by Cartier, the well-known jeweller.

**FRENCH POCKETKNIFE PATTERNS** France boasts an ancient cutlery industry and a wide array of traditional pocketknife patterns. Best known today are the Opinels from Cognin. Standard Opinels, sold worldwide, are wood-handled penny knives with a rotating ferrule lock. De luxe horn- and ivory-handled models made for collectors are sold by Courty et Fils in Paris.

Almost as familiar is the Laguiole, a locking clasp knife with a slender yatagan-style blade, and often with a corkscrew in the back. Pierre Calmels makes the genuine article in the town of Laguiole (his grandfather created the pattern there), but the best-known export Laguioles come from G. David.

The French pradel, named after a 19th-century family of Thiers cutlers, is strikingly similar to the most basic American jack knife, the barlow, named after a 17th-century family of Sheffield cutlers. "Pradel" is the name for a barehead regular jack with a single short-pull spear blade, and "pradel" is also the French name for this blade.

The Mediterranean island of Corsica, which is French territory, boasts its own distinctive style of "Vendetta Corse" folding knives. These self-guard clasp knives with long bolsters have deadly needle-sharp blades, and are made both in Thiers and on Corsica in a wide range of sizes.

**GERMAN POCKETKNIFE PATTERNS** For a millennium German cutlers were swordsmiths to the world, and for more than a century they were pocket cutlers to the world as well. Endless varieties of pocketknives were made in Solingen for export, with a much more limited variety made for German domestic sale.

Most typical of Germany's own pocketknives are the large stag-handled folding hunters. These were made in multiple sizes and shapes, and with a multiplicity of auxiliary blades – usually a saw and a corkscrew.

Also typical was the clasp knife with horn or stag or deer-foot handle (the latter complete with fur and hoof), which was the ancestor of the American pattern called the tickler or toothpick. An inexpensive all-metal version of this knife, made by Kauffmann, has been popular in Germany since World War I.

## TRADITIONAL JAPANESE POCKETKNIFE
PATTERNS Today most of the pocketknives made in Japan are copied from American or European prototypes, but Japan does have its own traditional style of folding knife. This all-metal Higonokami knife boasts a laminated steel blade with a cut-off point and super-sharp cutting edge. The blade is sabre ground on the front and flat on the back. High-quality examples are signed by the maker with a calligraphic flourish both on the flat of the blade and on the steel handle.

During World War II some Japanese pilots carried inexpensive all-metal figural knives embossed with low-relief images of Japanese aircraft. I have seen half a dozen different types, but these are very rare now, and largely forgotten in Japan.

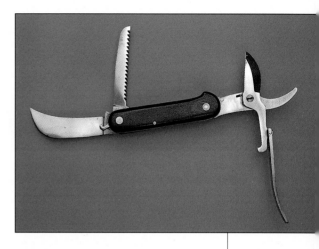

ABOVE
**Hoffritz (US retailer) German-made folding pruning knife with pruning blade, pruning shears, and pruning saw, wood handles.**

LEFT
**Stainless steel, Japan, equal-end lobster pen knife with stainless steel handles. Blades: spear master blade, scissors, manicure blade, folding cigarette lighter.**

# OAK LEAF POCKET KNIVES
## HOW THEY ARE MADE

**POCKET BLADES.**

No. 1—Pocket Blade, for No. K2420, Partially Forged; Showing Steel Bar from which it is being Fashioned.

No. 2—Pocket Blade Forged, Ready for Hardening and Tempering or Grinding.

No. 3—Pocket Blade Ground, Ready for Drilling and Filing, or Drilling and Squaring.

No. 4—Pocket Blade Ready for assembling. Filed and Dressed, or Drilled, Squared and Dressed.

**PEN BLADES.**

No. 1—Pen Blade for No. K2420, Partially Forged; Showing Steel Bar from which it is being Fashioned.

No. 2—Pen Blade Forged, Ready for Hardening and Tempering or Grinding.

No. 3—Pen Blade Ground, Ready for Drilling and Filing, or Drilling and Squaring.

No. 4—Pen Blade Ready for Assembling. Drilled, Filed and Dressed, or Drilled, Squared and Dressed.

No. 5—Spring Steel, from which Spring is Produced.

No. 6—Spring, Dressed and Drilled, Ready for Adjusting.

No. 7—Spring Adjusted, Filed, Hardened, Tempered and Dressed.

No. 8—Sheet Brass, from which Linings are Pressed.

No. 9—German Silver, from which Bolsters are made.

No. 10—Blank for Bolster, Pressed Ready for Stamping.

No. 11—Bolster Stamped up, Ready to Fasten to Lining.

No. 12—Brass Strip, Pierced, Ready to Receive Bolster.

No. 13—Bolsters "Chopped on" Lining, Ready for Passing through Pattern Dies.

No. 14—Scale Pressed, Ready for Drilling.

No. 15—Handle Covering, Ready for Fitting.

No. 16—Covering Fitted, Ready for Name Plate.

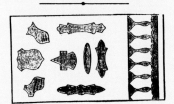

No. 17—Name Plates, or Shields, and German Silver from which they are made.

No. 18—Scales, with Covering Fitted, Showing Name Plate and Reverse Side, Ready for Assembling into Handle.

No. 19—Division Scale, or Center Lining.

No. 20—Knife Ready for Final Adjusting—Note Loose Rivets and General Rough Appearance of Knife.

# CHAPTER III

# MAKING POCKETKNIVES

These drawings from a *circa* 1910 catalogue of the E. C. Simmons Hardware Company show how a typical equal-end jack knife of that time was made, in the firm's own Walden Knife Co factory. OAK LEAF and KEEN KUTTER were the principal Simmons house brands. What these drawings do not reveal is the people, the machinery, and the processes involved in performing all these steps.

The first step in manufacture was forging the blades from carbon steel strip (1,2). In American shops this was generally a punch press operation, while in Sheffield in that period it was still usually done by hand. The forged blades were then die cut to shape and heat treated, after which the tangs were drilled, the surfaces ground, and the flats of the tang filed (3,4). Today, the hole in the tang is punched in the same operation that gives the blade its final profile. Springs were produced in much the same way as blades, except that they were not forged before being die cut (5–7).

In another part of the factory, the parts for the frame were made. Chunks of nickel silver or mild steel were die cut from thick stock, and then stamped or "coined" in a press to form the

No. 21—The Finished Article.

ABOVE
**E. C. Simmons Oak Leaf equal-end jackknife.**

LEFT
**The manufacture of an Oak Leaf pocketknife.**

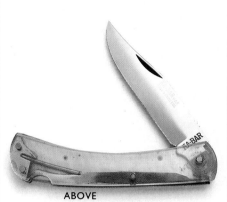

**Ka-Bar 1189 folding hunter, cutaway demonstrator model. Note internal music-wire spring.**

**Unmarked (usually Sheffield made) "escape knife" made for the US Office of Strategic Services, World War II.**

bolsters, usually with a stud projecting from the inner surface (9–11). Properly spaced holes were then drilled in strips of brass, and pairs of bolsters were "chopped on" to these (12,13). Then these strips were passed through the "Pattern Dies", which cut out the final shape of the knife's handle (14,8). The resulting frame piece was called a "scale". Nearby, the shield (17) and the centre liner (19) were also cut out.

Meanwhile, in another department the "handle covers" had been prepared from wood, bone, ivory, pearl, stag, or a synthetic material (15). These covers were fitted to the scales, and the front cover was inletted to receive the shield (16). Next, holes were drilled for rivets: one in each bolster, one in each end of the cover, two in the shield (18), and one in the bottom centre, to anchor the spring. The handle rivets and shield rivets were then set.

Next the knife was assembled (20) and given to a cutler, who was responsible for final fit and adjustment of "walk and talk" – smooth operation and a positive snap upon opening and closing. The blades were final-polished, honed, and etched (21), and the finished knives were oiled, wrapped, and boxed in half dozens.

············ FACTORS AND FACTORIES ··············
Originally the word "factory" meant the warehouse of a factor. A factor was primarily a merchant, who, in the knife trade, commissioned independent cutlers (in Sheffield they were called "little mesters") to make knives for him marked with his name. Each cutler specialized in one or two patterns, or in just a single operation, such as forging, grinding, hafting (putting on handles), or cutlering (final assembly and adjustment).

This system of outside contracting or outworking was standard in Sheffield, Solingen, and Seki City, Japan (where it is still the norm). It provided an efficient allocation of labour and resources, but it meant uncertain employment for labour, and uncertain supply of labour for the factors. To combat these disadvantages, some factors converted their "factories" – their warehouses – into factories in the modern sense, large workshops where all operations were carried out under one roof, either by employees or by inside contractors.

The first pocketknife factories in the world were set up in France in the 18th century. Using water-powered machinery,

## SEQUENCE BOARDS

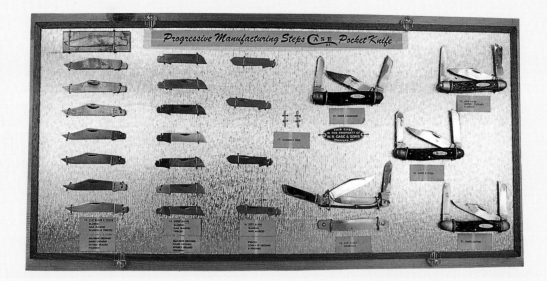

One of the oldest sales aids in cutlers' shops is the "sequence of manufacture" board. A sequence board is a series of identical knives, or the component parts thereof, each one carried one step nearer to completion than the previous one. The first steps in a sequence board usually show the cutler's raw materials: bars or strips of steel, nickel silver, and brass, often along with assorted handle materials. The last step is usually the finished cutlery item. In between, each piece or assembly fixed to the board demonstrates one or more stages in the manufacturing process.

These boards were used to sell individual knives to consumers, as well as the manufacturer's entire line of knives to retailers. Many manufacturers and distributors displayed sequence boards in their factory showrooms and regional sales offices, and in their showcases of wares on exhibit at expositions, trade shows, and world fairs. Original sequence boards are one of the items most sought by knife collectors.

This sequence board from W. R. Case & Sons of Bradford, Pennsylvania, is shown here courtesy of its present owner, Smoky Mountain Knife Works in Sevierville, Tennessee, which has hundreds of antique cutlery advertising items on public display.

they mass-produced inexpensive "penny knives", folding knives without backsprings.

In Sheffield, the first modern factory was the "Sheaf Works" of William Greaves & Sons, built between 1823 and 1826. Best known in the US was the "Washington Works" of George Wostenholm & Son. First occupied by that firm in 1848, it was pulled down in 1971 to make way for a car park. The last large Sheffield cutlery factory, built for Richards Brothers in 1946, was demolished in 1984.

The first modern pocket cutlery factory in Solingen was built in 1805 by a factor named Peter Daniel Peres. Although Solingen has since acquired many large factories, the system of outworking

TOP
**The Victorinox factory in Ibach, Switzerland.**

BOTTOM
**One of the many stages in assembling Victorinox "Swiss Army" knives.**

and independent cutlers still survives there.

The first modern cutlery factory in the US was built by John Russell in Greenfield, Massachusetts, in 1834. He was inspired in this endeavour by an account of Sheffield methods he had read in a book, *The Practical Tourist* by Zachariah Allen. Perhaps coincidentally, the amount of Sheffield cutlery sold in the United States peaked at over 50 per cent the following year.

The first recorded pocketknife factory in the US was Lyman Bradley & Co of Naugatuck, Connecticut, in 1841. A few years later Bradley was one of the managers of the fledgling Waterville Mfg Co in nearby Waterbury, which soon had 200 mainly Sheffield-trained employees making pocketknives. Lyman Bradley remained active in the cutlery industry until the 1890s.

**LARGEST IN THE WORLD** The construction of large cutlery factories led naturally to rivalry over which was the biggest. The Sheaf Works was the first in Sheffield, but it was soon surpassed in size by many others. In 1850 the largest cutlery factory in Sheffield – and in the world – was No 6 Norfolk Street, the works of Joseph Rodgers & Sons.

By 1870 the title had crossed the Atlantic to the US. J. Russell & Co's new plant at Turners Falls, Massachusetts, now the largest cutlery factory in the world, continued to grow, adding a pocketknife division in 1875.

By 1900 the title had moved to the Aetna Works of Landers, Frary & Clark, founded in New Britain, Connecticut, in 1865. This firm made no pocketknives until 1912, when it took over neighbouring Humason & Beckley (founded 1853). From 1914 until the 1930s, H. & B.'s staff and facilities made L. F. & C. UNIVERSAL brand pocketknives. The Aetna Works were demolished in 1965, and today the world's largest cutlery factory is Imperial Schrade's 500,000 square foot (46,000m²) facility in Ellenville, New York.

···· MULTI-BLADES AND GADGET KNIVES ····
For almost as long as cutlers have been making folding knives, they have been working out ways to include other tools with the cutting blades in their knives' handles. The first step was to include more than one blade, either as insurance against breakage, or to perform a specialized cutting task such as

## FOLDING KNIVES
. . . . . . . . . . . . . .

These are some of the blades and tools used in folding knives:

Leather punch ● Harness mending bolts ● Belt punch ● Gimlet ● Awl ● Typesetter's punch ● Quill pen blade ● Pen machine ● Letter opener ● Marlinespike ● Rope blade ● Weaver's hook ● Seam ripper ● Button hook ● Manicure blade and file ● Corn blade ● Scissors ● Spatula or palette knife ● Saw for bone and wood ● Metal saw ● Cockspur saw ● Spey blade ● Castrating hook ● Seton needle ● Scalpel or bistoury ● Fleam ● Hoof-pick ● Dog stripping comb ● Horticultural budding and grafting blade ● Grafting spud ● Cotton sampling blade ● Maize blade ● Pruning hook ● Pruning shears ● Weed digger ● Cigar cutter ● Cigar punch ● Cigar stub fork ● Cigar box opener ● Cigar box hammer ● Pipe tamper ● Pipe bowl reamer ● Snuff box ● Game counter ● Dice cup with miniature dice ● Silver or gold fruit blade ● Silver or gold nut and seed pick ● Fork ● Spoon ● Ear spoon ● Corkscrew ● Cork-pulling hook ● Champagne wire-cutter ● Oyster opener ● Tin-opener ● Bottle cap lifter ● Screwdriver ● Pliers ● Electrical wire stripper ● Wire-cutter ● Crescent wrench ● Alligator wrench ● Fuse cutter ● Dynamite cap crimper ● "Pres-to-lite" key (for early car headlights) ● Key blank ● Skeleton key ● Carriage key ● Key-ring ● Ruler ● Tape measure ● Feeler gauges ● Pen or pencil ● Pencil sharpener ● Ink eraser blade ● Drawing compass ● Magnetic compass ● Whistle ● Siren ● Magnifying glass ● Stanhope lens with miniature photos ● Race ● Fish scaler ● Fish gaff ● Spring balance ● Hook disgorger ● Hook hone ● Fly-tying vise ● Shotgun shell extractors ● Shotgun choke tube wrench ● Skinning blade ● Gutting blade ● Bird gutting-hook ● Hatchet or cleaver ● Dagger blade ● Pistol ● Pinfire blank pistol

**Pull-out implements in handle**
Toothpick ● Tweezers ● Lancet ● Dividers ● Cigar punch ● Fly-tying vise ● Sharpening steel

**Interchangeable Blades for "Tool Kit Knives"** Cutting blades ● Files ● Saws ● Screwdrivers ● Gimlet ● Punch ● Chisel ● Ruler ● Tin- and bottle-openers ● Cork pullers ● Hammer

ABOVE
**Latima, Italy, pocket-watch/knife, stainless steel handles.**

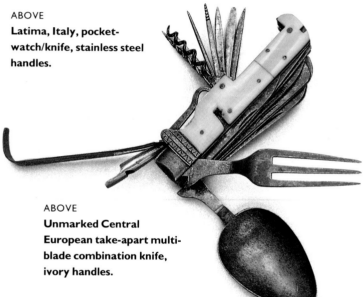

ABOVE
**Unmarked Central European take-apart multi-blade combination knife, ivory handles.**

sharpening a quill pen.

The most obvious non-blade tool first to be included in pocketknives was the leather punch, a sharp tool essential for mending broken harnesses.

By the 18th century, master cutlers were including a wide array of specialized blades and tools in folding knives. The ultimate was Joseph Rodgers & Sons "Year Knife", begun in 1822 with 1,822 different blades, which had one more blade added to it every year until about 1970. Of course most of those blades were duplicates, but there are fancy horseman's and sportsman's knives with forty to fifty distinct blades and other tools. Today both Victorinox and Wenger of Switzerland make de luxe "Swiss Army" knives with up to two dozen different blades and tools.

# THE MOST POPULAR BRANDS OF POCKETKNIVES

A knife is a knife. So why do collectors care so much about the brand names on knives? There are two reasons.

First, some people make knives better than others do, so brands can reflect quality. Also, the brand on a knife can indicate its approximate age. It can tell you how it fits into the larger world: where and when it was made, where and how it was sold — mail order, hardware shop, cutlery shop, jewellery shop, department store, sporting goods shop, itinerant peddler, promotional item, and so on — and even what sort of person might have bought it originally.

Brands also matter to those who like to collect things in complete sets. A knife's brand can tell them if it "belongs" with their other knives.

········ FAMOUS AMERICAN BRANDS ··········

**CASE BROTHERS/W. R. CASE & SONS** Case brand pocketknives have been the most popular among American collectors for more than twenty-five years. In fact, two principal companies made Case knives: Case Brothers, and W. R. Case & Sons.

ABOVE
**Case XX folding hunter, red bone stag.**

# W. R. CASE & SONS  BLADE TANG STAMPINGS

What lies behind the popularity of the Case brand? One key factor is that in the late 1960s and early 1970s, when pocketknife collecting first became popular, Case still offered a diverse high-quality line of traditional pocketknife patterns, some with de luxe natural handles such as pearl and stag. Those knives were widely available, thanks to one of the best sales teams in the business.

After a 1972 corporate buy-out, Case's assets, sales personnel, and good will disappeared, but somehow the firm survives, independent again, and has even begun a renaissance.

Another factor in collector popularity is that Case changed its blade tang stampings over the years in a fairly systematic fashion, which allows collectors readily to date them. In particular, a most noticeable marking change had been made in 1965, and many of the older "Double X" knives were still in stock in retail inventories in the early 1970s.

Since 1896 more than 75 tang stampings have been used by cutlery firms owned or founded by members of the Case family. Most are very rare and of interest only to advanced collectors. The basic W. R. Case & Sons markings are listed below.

**W. R. CASE & SONS/BRADFORD PA.** This is still the company name, but it was used as a two-line tang stamping from about 1905 to about 1920. (Some recent reissue "collector" knives also bear this stamping, but their materials and finish identify them as modern.)

**CASE/TESTED XX.** (Usually with the "C" larger than the other letters, and often continued to form an underline beneath the "ASE".) Called by collectors "Circle C" or "Tested", this mark, in several slight variations, was standard from about 1920 to 1940 or 1941. Beware; this mark is now widely counterfeited.

**CASE/XX.** Called "Double X" by collectors, this two-line mark was standard on Case pocketknives from the postwar resumption of commercial marketing in 1945 through 1965.

**CASE XX/MADE IN U.S.A.** 1965–1970. Called "Case USA" by collectors. In 1917 and 1918 Case stamped MADE IN U.S.A. in a circle on the sailor knives that it sold to the US Navy, but had otherwise not used this designation. Then, in 1965, the Canadian Government began to require that imported goods be marked to show country of origin (a US requirement since 1891). Because Case sold many knives in Canada – it had even run a factory in Pictou, Nova Scotia, in the late 1940s – the firm changed all of its blade markings to comply.

**CASE XX/MADE IN U.S.A./** above a row of tiny dots. 1970 to 1980. The dots indicate the year of manufacture (10 dots = 1970; 9 dots = 1971; etc). In 1970 Case began to cater to collectors, hoping that this dating code would encourage collectors to buy a full set of Case knives every year. For a time the strategy worked, but the Case line was shortened after 1972 and its quality declined. Many collectors lost interest, but those who still care call these knives "ten-dot", "nine-dot", and so on.

**CASE XX/ row of dots with runic SS in centre/ U.S.A.** 1980–1990 (10 dots = 1980; 9 dots = 1981; etc). Called "Lightning S" by collectors. The runic "SS" means "Stainless Steel".

**CASE XX/BRADFORD PA./\*USA\*.** The current Case mark.

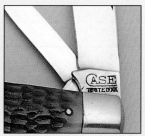

1905 – 1920          1920 – 1940/41          1945 – 1965          1980 – 1990

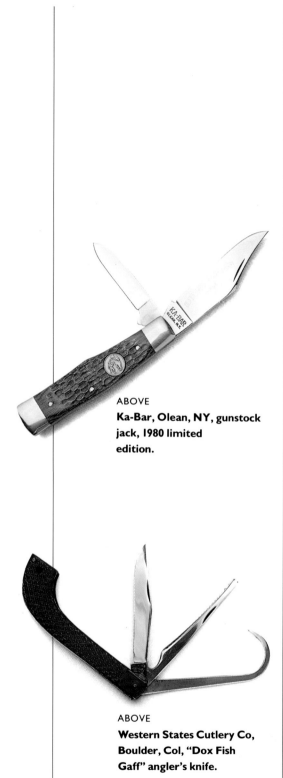

ABOVE

**Ka-Bar, Olean, NY, gunstock jack, 1980 limited edition.**

ABOVE

**Western States Cutlery Co, Boulder, Col, "Dox Fish Gaff" angler's knife.**

In 1896 three brothers named Jean, John, and Andrew Case began a wholesale cutlery firm in Little Valley, New York. Their Case Bros brand pocketknives were at first contract-made by C. Platts & Sons (see below). In 1900 Case Brothers began to manufacture their own pocketknives, along with straight razors and hones. This firm continued until 1915.

In 1902 a nephew of the three Case brothers, J. Russell Case, opened his own cutlery jobbing firm in Little Valley. J. R. named his firm W. R. Case & Sons Cutlery Co, after his father, William Russell Case, elder brother of Jean, John, and Andrew, although W. R. Case was in fact never involved in the cutlery business. In 1905 J. Russell Case, together with H. N. Platts, opened a factory for W. R. Case & Sons in Bradford, Pennsylvania, about twenty miles from Little Valley. "Case" knives from this factory excite great interest among collectors today.

### C. W. PLATTS & SONS/WESTERN STATES CUTLERY CO.

In 1864, Sheffield cutler Charles W. Platts emigrated to the United States. He worked for the American Knife Company until 1872, when he was hired as superintendent of the Northfield Knife Company, like American Knife in Connecticut. During his 24 years at Northfield, he brought his five sons in as apprentice cutlers. In 1896 the Platts family started its own pocketknife firm, C. W. Platts & Sons, in upstate New York, and moved to Eldred, Pennsylvania, the following year.

C. W. Platts died in 1900, and his second son, Harvey Nixon Platts, took over management of the firm. In 1905 H. N. Platts and his brother-in-law J. Russell Case of the jobbing firm W. R. Case & Sons Cutlery Co joined forces to build a new factory in Bradford, Pennsylvania, using the better-known W. R. Case & Sons brand name.

In 1911 H. N. Platts sold his interest in Case and, for health reasons, moved to Boulder, Colorado. There he started Western States Cutlery & Mfg Company, which was strictly a jobbing firm until 1920, when Platts began the first pocketknife firm manufacturing in the West. In 1928 the company added hunting knives to its product selection. From 1956 to 1984 the firm was called Western Cutlery Co; from 1984 to 1990 it was Coleman-Western.

The Western States brand products most in demand among collectors are pocketknives with the master blade etched TESTED SHARP TEMPER in a "noughts-and-crosses" grid, which were made prior to 1941.

**UNION CUTLERY CO/KA-BAR** In around 1890 brothers Wallace and Emerson Brown began to manufacture and import pocketknives and razors as Brown Bros Mfg Co in Tidioute, Pennsylvania. In 1898 they adopted the name Union Razor Co; in 1909 this name was changed to Union Cutlery Co. The firm moved to a new factory in Olean, New York, in 1912.

Wallace Brown was married to Emma Case, a sister of W. R. Case, and so Union and the various Case firms worked together closely. In 1923 Union adopted the trademark KA-BAR, an acronym for "Case Brothers". Under this name its pocketknives and hunting knives grew popular and widely known. The front handle of some of the larger Union Cutlery KA-BARs are inlaid with a shield in the shape of a dog's head.

The name KA-BAR is commonly associated with the US Marine Corps 1219C2 (Navy Mark 2) combat knife, introduced in 1943. Although developed and primarily contracted by Camillus, more than a million of these knives bore the prominent KA-BAR stamping – hence the popular name for the type. Camillus and KA-BAR versions of this knife are still sold commercially.

Union Cutlery's name was changed to Kabar Cutlery Co in 1951, a watershed date for collectors, because later stampings are much less desirable. The trademark was then modernized to *Kabar*, although the older "KA-BAR" is still occasionally used on limited edition reissues of classic knives. Since 1966 Kabar Cutlery has been a division of Cole National Corp in Cleveland, Ohio (other brands: Khyber, Sabre, Monarch). Most current Kabar brand knives are contract-made, and the rest are imported.

**CATTARAUGUS CUTLERY CO/KINFOLKS INC**
These firms began as J. B. F. Champlin & Son of Little Valley, New York, in 1882, wholesale importers of German cutlery. In 1886 its founder, John Brown Francis Champlin, and his son, Tint, changed the company's name to Cattaraugus, the name of the county of which Little Valley is the seat, and began

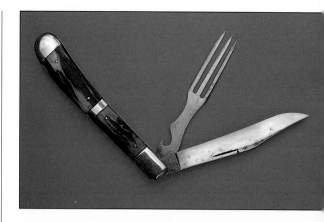

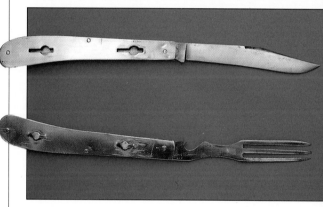

ABOVE
**Union Cutlery Co, Olean, NY, Model 2291K&F "slot knife" take-apart knife and fork, genuine stag handles.**

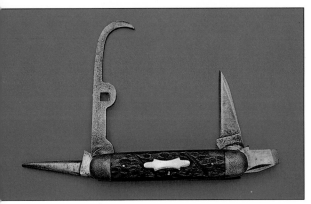

TOP
**Cattaraugus Cutlery Co, Little Valley, NY, crescent wrench knife, bone stag handles.**

BOTTOM
**Robeson Cutlery Co, Rochester, NY, multi-blade wagon knife with spear master blade (worn down), stubby screwdriver, patent punch, and combination hoof-pick/Pres-to-lite (headlight) key blade, bone stag handles.**

ABOVE
**Robeson No-Rustain lockback English jack with folding guard.**

manufacturing cutlery locally as a supplement to their imports. John Champlin died in 1903, Tint in 1938. Their firm survived until 1963.

In its early years Cattaraugus mainly sold pocketknives, razors, and scissors, adding hunting knives in 1925. The hunting knives were made in the Kinfolks factory, also in Little Valley. Kinfolks, begun as a joint venture between Case and Cattaraugus, later became independent. It also made pocketknives.

During World War II the main Cattaraugus products were stout 225Q "commando" knives, aircrew survival folding machetes, and TL-29 electrician's knives (the "liner lock" on these was a 1906 Cattaraugus invention). In the 1930s the firm made all of the knives for Admiral Richard E. Byrd's Antarctic expeditions. After World War II Cattaraugus mainly made fixed-blade kitchen knives with black plastic handles and chrome-plated blades. Cattaraugus was a popular brand to collect ten or fifteen years ago, but its popularity has faded.

**ROBESON CUTLERY CO** Like so many others, this cutlery firm began as a wholesaler. Millard Robeson sold imported knives from his home in Elmira, New York. In 1894 he began to manufacture knives in Charles Sherwood's plant in Camillus, New York. In 1898 Robeson built his own factories in Rochester and Perry, New York, to make "*Shuredge*" brand pocketknives. A third factory was added in Mt Morris, New York, during World War I.

Emerson Case (son of J. Russell Case, and grandson of W. R. Case) was president of Robeson from 1940 to 1965 and led the firm to its greatest prosperity. Emerson Case introduced the sub-zero quench of stainless steel blades, now universally used. In 1965, upon Case's retirement, Robeson ceased manufacturing, but it continued to sell contract-made Robeson knives until 1977. Although popular with collectors, Robeson knives are much less in demand and less valuable than others, such as Case or KA-BAR.

**REMINGTON U.M.C./PAL BLADE CO** On 9 February, 1920, the Remington Arms – Union Metallic Cartridge Company assembled its first pocketknife in its large

ABOVE
**Remington 1993 "Bullet" knife.**

ABOVE
**Remington "Bullet" R4466 double-end trapper, genuine stag handles.**

## REMINGTON BULLETS

R1123 4½ inch (11.25 cm) larger trapper, bone ● R1128 4½ inch (11.25 cm) large trapper, wood ● R1173 "Baby Bullet", 3½ inch (9.75 cm) large trapper, bone ● R1253 5½ inch (13.75 cm) curved regular lockback hunting knife, bone ● R1263 5⅜ inch (13.5 cm) curved regular jack, clip master blade, bone ● R1273 5⅜ inch (13.5 cm) curved regular jack, spear master blade, bone ● R1306 4⅝ inch (11.5m) swell-centre hunting knife, stag ● R1303 4½ inch (11.25 cm) swell-centre hunting knife, bone ● R1613 5 inch (12.5 cm) tickler, bone ● R4243 4¾ inch (11.9 cm) large four-blade utility knife, bone ● R4353 4¼ inch (10.6 cm) double-end trapper, bone ● R4466 5⅜ inch (13.5 cm) double-end trapper, stag.

Bridgeport, Connecticut, factory. This ultra-modern plant had made ammunition for the Allied armies in France during World War I, and by 1925 Remington's cutlery division had grown to be the dominant maker of top-quality pocketknives in the United States.

At its peak in 1931, Remington was making over 10,000 high-quality pocketknives per day. The full product selection included over 1,000 pocketknife patterns, along with hunting knives and household cutlery, plus an unprecedented array of advertising and promotional materials which today are as collectible as the pocketknives.

On 12 November, 1940, Remington stopped cutlery production abruptly to resume defence work, and the firm's cutlery tooling and parts were sold to the Pal Blade Company of Plattsburgh, New York.

Collectors have long favoured Remington knives, in part because of the famous name that links with gun collecting, and in part because the older generation remembers Remington as the most desirable brand of knives from the days of their youth. Today Remington is one of the most sought-after brands of all.

**REMINGTON BULLETS** In September 1922 Remington introduced the first two of a dozen patterns of large stout sportsman's folding knives, each with a shield in the shape of high-power rifle cartridge – hence the collector name for these knives: "Remington Bullets". The initial "bullet" knife, and by far the most popular (and still the most common) was the R1123 large trapper with jigged bone handles. Its companion was the wood-handled version of this pattern, designated R1128. This pattern had been a German design, brought over to the US before World War I by C. W. Tillmanns, the Solingen cutler whom Remington had hired in 1919 to manage its cutlery production.

The R1128 and the other ten "bullets" are today much scarcer than the R1123. Rare variants of blade etch, bone jigging, and other details add challenge for advanced collectors, but there are just twelve basic bullet knife patterns. These are listed in the box on the left.

In 1940 Remington abandoned the cutlery business, but in 1982 Remington Arms commissioned Camillus Cutlery Co to make replicas of the R1123 "bullet" large trapper with Delrin plastic handles as part of a promotion for a new rifle. The knife

ABOVE
**Pal Blade Co, Plattsburgh, NY, easy-open swell-end jack, bronze handles, with leftover Remington pen blade (made c1940–1942).**

ABOVE
**Winchester, New Haven, Conn, Model 1920 swell-centre folding hunter, bone stag handles.**

RIGHT
**Winchester 2877 muskrat.**

attracted far more interest than the gun, and since then Remington has issued a new replica "bullet" knife every year, along with a colourful poster. Some of these reissues are now nearly as rare and valuable as the original Remington "bullet" knives, and knives made by other firms which were modelled on the R1123 and R1306 are popular with some "bullet" knife collectors. Remington also offers a short line of contract-made pocketknives through cutlery and sporting goods shops.

**WINCHESTER/NAPANOCH/EAGLE** Remington was not the only firearms firm to enter the cutlery business after World War I. Rival Winchester, in New Haven, Connecticut, followed a different strategy, and had even more ambitious goals. Remington intended to dominate the cutlery industry – and did so – but Winchester set its sights on the entire hardware trade.

Remington hired experienced cutlers to design and install a brand-new facility, while Winchester bought existing cutlery firms and moved staff and equipment to New Haven in 1919. Napanoch Knife Co of Napanoch, New York, (founded 1901, and a major private brand contractor) provided a cadre of skilled cutlers and a range of premium patterns. Eagle Knife Co of New Haven, founded in 1916 by the Hemming Brothers who had invented the first successful automatic grinder in 1903 (many are still in use), provided the technology for modern mass production.

# REVOLUTION GOES UNDERGROUND

When Remington and Winchester got into the pocketknife business after World War I, both firms experimented with modernizing the manufacturing processes. Winchester tried to do away with forging in their first blades, substituting blanked and ground chrome-vanadium tool steel (with superior edge-holding characteristics) for forged high-carbon steel. Remington, meanwhile, tried to do away with the extra steps and uncertain results of "chopping on" bolsters to liners by substituting integral drop-forged handle frames.

Both firms' innovations ran into a brick wall, however, in the form of a group of tradition-minded individuals: professional hardware buyers. "New" brand names could just barely be tolerated, particularly since Remington and Winchester were both well known in the gun business; new pocketknife technology, on the other hand, they would not countenance. So Winchester went back to forged blades, and Remington went back to assembled handle frames except in their later R-100 series of integral frame "Dollar Knives".

Both firms did continue to develop new technology, but thenceforth made sure that it did not show. Today pocketknife firms continue to hide most of their technological innovations under a veneer of traditional appearance.

Winchester's next step was distribution. While Remington was selling through regional hardware houses, Winchester merged with the largest national hardware wholesaler in the US, E. C. Simmons of St Louis, Missouri. Winchester-Simmons then embarked upon an aggressive programme of franchising established hardware retailers as "Winchester Stores", stocked with a full range of Winchester brand merchandise. This innovative pattern of hardware distribution was ahead of its time in the 1920s, but is standard practice today. Then in 1930 Winchester and Simmons divorced. Winchester continued to make knives until the US entry into World War II, late in 1941.

Original Winchester pocketknives are very nearly the quality of Remingtons (except for the cheap "assortment knives", made as a supplementary line during the Great Depression of the 1930s). Winchesters are as popular among collectors as Remingtons, and they are equally valuable.

**RE-ISSUE WINCHESTERS** In about 1985 Winchester authorized Blue Grass Cutlery Co, a small wholesale firm in Manchester, Ohio, to sell new knives branded with the Winchester trademark. Most of these new Winchester knives are made by Queen Cutlery Co in traditional patterns with natural handle materials, while a few others are made by Utica and by Camillus. These reissue Winchesters are attractive, well-made knives, with a devoted following among collectors.

In addition, both Winchester-Germany and Winchester-France, national distribution agencies for Winchester firearms, offer modern-style knives marked with the Winchester logo. These knives are made in Germany, Italy, and Japan, and are not sold in the US, but are widely available in Europe.

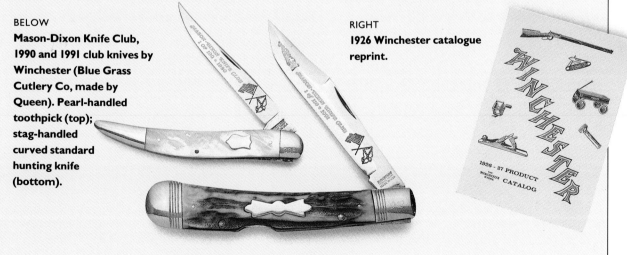

BELOW
**Mason-Dixon Knife Club, 1990 and 1991 club knives by Winchester (Blue Grass Cutlery Co, made by Queen). Pearl-handled toothpick (top); stag-handled curved standard hunting knife (bottom).**

RIGHT
**1926 Winchester catalogue reprint.**

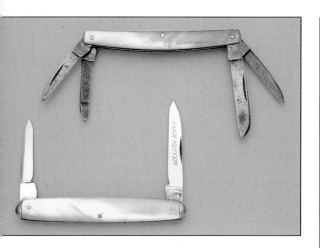

ABOVE
**Two E. C. Simmons Keen Kutter pearl-handled pen knives: a four-blade shadow congress (top), and a senator with tip bolsters (bottom).**

ABOVE
**New York Knife Co, Walden, NY, dog figural knife, carved pearl handles.**

## E. C. SIMMONS – KEEN KUTTER/WALDEN KNIFE CO

Of the hundreds of wholesale hardware firms in the United States, the best known and most successful was the E. C. Simmons Hardware Co of St. Louis, Missouri, established in 1868 as successor to an older firm. In 1874, Simmons became the first hardware firm to be incorporated – to allow employee profit-sharing – and it was the first wholesaler to produce an illustrated catalogue (in 1881). While other hardware merchants were developing their regional markets, Edward Campbell Simmons was working nationwide. Others contracted with cutlery and tool firms for private brand merchandise; Simmons bought up key manufacturers, to control both the costs and the supply of his KEEN KUTTER and OAK LEAF brands and to make a profit selling private-brand merchandise to other firms.

Simmons acquired the Walden Knife Co, Walden, New York, in 1902. This pocket cutlery firm had been founded circa 1870 by a group of New York Knife Co employees who had resigned in a dispute over a company baseball game. Walden made the Simmons KEEN KUTTER knives. Other Simmons pocketknife brands from various sources, mainly in Germany, included HORNET, WILLIAM ENDERS OAK LEAF, and SIMMONS HARDWARE CO.

E. C. Simmons died in 1921, at the age of 82. The following year his successors merged Simmons with the Winchester Repeating Arms Co (page 35). Walden Knife Co was closed the following year, and its staff and equipment moved to New Haven.

In 1930 Simmons and Winchester separated. A decade later, Simmons was absorbed by its long-time St Louis rival, Shapleigh Hardware Co (established 1843). KEEN KUTTER then became Shapleigh's budget brand (Shapleigh's KEEN KUTTER knives are not marked E. C. SIMMONS). Shapleigh closed its doors in 1960, and its premium DIAMOND EDGE brand was sold to Imperial.

## NEW YORK KNIFE CO

New York Knife Co grew to be one of the largest and most successful of the many New York and Connecticut pocketknife firms started by Sheffield emigrés in the mid-19th century. Founded in Matteawan (now Beacon) in 1852 and relocated to Walden in 1856, the firm owed much of its success to its second generation president, Thomas W. Bradley,

ABOVE
**New York Knife Co, Walden, NY, (Hammer Brand) Model 135 rase knife (timber scriber) with cocobolo handles.**

ABOVE
**Queen Cutlery Co, Titusville, Pa, sleeveboard jack, Winterbottom bone handles.**

ABOVE
**Queen Cutlery Co, Titusville, Pa, limited edition cock-fighting knife with spear master blade, cockspur saw, and string hook.**

Jr, a Medal of Honor winner in the Civil War, and a US congressman after 1903. An officer in Orange County's 124th "Orange Blossom" Volunteer Regiment, Bradley named his de luxe gunstock lobster whittler pattern the "Orange Blossom" in its honour.

Before Remington entered the cutlery market in 1920, New York Knife Co was the leading supplier of high-quality pocketknives to hardware wholesalers, both under its own HAMMER BRAND (first used *c*1880) and under a myriad of house brand names. *Circa* 1911, New York Knife Co was the first US firm authorized to make Official Boy Scout knives. Beginning in 1928 the firm also sold cheap mass-produced knives bearing the brand WALLKILL RIVER WORKS, after the English-style formal name of the factory.

Although steadily losing market share to Remington, Winchester, Case, and other upstarts, New York Knife Co survived the 1920s. Then, in 1930, James Fuller, its president since 1916, tried an experiment. He organized an auction on 15 September to sell an entire year's output of pocketknives. It was a disaster and obliged New York Knife Co to go out of business a few months later. Its HAMMER BRAND logo was later acquired by Imperial.

### SCHATT & MORGAN/QUEEN CUTLERY CO

Like so many other knife company founders, J. W. Schatt and C. B. Morgan had begun as cutlery importers and jobbers. In 1895 they built a factory in Gowanda, New York, and sold it a year later to C. W. Platts. They relocated to Titusville, Pennsylvania – known as "The Queen City", and birthplace in 1859 of the American petroleum industry.

In 1922 several Schatt & Morgan supervisors started Queen City Cutlery Co in their spare time, using S & M components. They were caught and fired in 1928, but by then S & M was bankrupt, and Queen City took over its assets. Since 1945 the firm has been called Queen Cutlery Company. While Queen and S & M knives are popular with collectors, Queen is best known today as the contract manufacturer of some KA-BARS, most reissue Winchesters, and the Case Heritage series. Queen also makes reissue Schatt & Morgan knives for collectors.

BELOW
**Ulster Knife Co, Ellenville, NY, senator pen, tip bolsters, bail to hang knife from watch chain, jigged bone handles.**

ABOVE
**Kingston (joint venture of Ulster and Imperial) utility knife made for the US Army, World War II.**

**J. RUSSELL & CO** In 1834 young John Russell built one of the first recorded cutlery factories in the United States, the Green River Works in Greenfield, Massachusetts. His products included butcher knives, table cutlery, and wood chisels. The firm grew, and in 1870 it was relocated to a new industrial development in Turners Falls, Mass. Five years later, J. Russell & Co began to make pocketknives. The line was complete for that time, but its best-known component was the Russell barlow knives.

The original barlow knives had been made by cutlers named Barlow(e) in 17th-century Sheffield. By the 19th century their name had become generic, applied to low-priced standard jacks with extended front bolsters and, usually, smooth bone handle covers.

Russell barlows became so popular, especially in the South of America, that nearly every hardware and cutlery firm, no matter what other brands it sold, offered a selection.

Russell suspended pocketknife production in 1917, using the war as an excuse. Under public pressure they resumed production, very reluctantly, in 1924. In 1933, Russell merged with Harrington Cutlery and relocated to Southbridge, Mass, in 1938. Russell barlows were last made in 1941, although both replicas and counterfeits have been offered in recent years.

The first knife collector organization of modern times was the highly informal "Barlow Bearcats", created in 1950 by newspaper columnist Allan Trout of the Louisville, Kentucky, *Courier-Journal*. To be a "Barlow Bearcat", one needed only to own an authentic Russell barlow knife.

**COOPERATIVE KNIFE CO/ULSTER KNIFE CO/KINGSTON** In 1871 a group of Sheffield Cutlers formed the Cooperative Knife Co in Ellenville, Ulster County, New York. This firm suffered the ills of most co-op ventures, such as inflexibility and weak marketing. It failed in 1876, but was re-organized by local banker Dwight Divine as the Ulster Knife Co. Under Divine, Ulster became a leading private brand contractor of high-quality knives.

After World War I, his son, C. Dwight Divine, continued using traditional Sheffield-style hand methods and quality while the

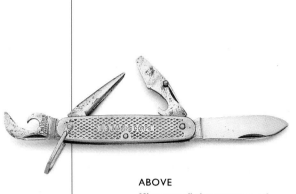

ABOVE
**Kingston (joint venture of Ulster and Imperial) utility knife made for the US Marine Corps, World War II.**

BELOW
**Imperial Dick Tracy character knife.**

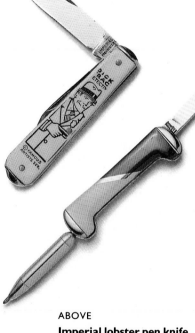

ABOVE
**Imperial lobster pen knife with Jackmaster (Lohr & Stiehl patent) sheet celluloid over hollow steel shell handles, folding ball-point pen.**

rest of the industry modernized. Divine matched his competitors' prices – and lost money every year from 1919 to 1941. In 1941 he sold Ulster to Albert M. Baer.

Baer gutted the factory and hired a young metallurgist from MIT named Edward Wallace, and a former Sears Roebuck buyer named Frank Kethcart. Together they quickly transformed Ulster into the most modern cutlery plant in the world.

After Pearl Harbor, Baer was selected to represent the cutlery industry on the Army Advisory Board of the Office of the Quartermaster General. The government suspended most anti-trust regulations, and all US cutlery firms were co-ordinated by the Board to make millions of knives for the armed forces. In 1943 Baer formed a joint venture with the owners of Imperial Knife Co, which they called Kingston Cutlery Co (Kingston was an old Ulster brand, named after the county seat of Ulster County). After the war Kingston took over Schrade Cutlery Co of Walden, New York, and the combined firm became Imperial Knife Associated Companies.

**IMPERIAL KNIFE CO** Sheffield and Solingen were not the only Old World cutlery centres to send cutlers to the US. In 1916, two brothers from Frosolone, Italy, Michael and Felix Mirando, who had been working for Empire Knife Co in Connecticut, started their own pocketknife firm in the American jewellery manufacturing centre, Providence, Rhode Island. At first they made "skeleton knives", which the jewellery firms would fit with gold or silver handles. In 1917 and 1918 they made vast numbers of little IKCO brand jack knives for the US Navy.

In 1919 Dominic Fazzano joined the firm. In the 1920s and early 1930s, Imperial specialized in low-cost mass-produced jack knives with fancy multi-coloured celluloid "pretty handles", popular today with cost-conscious collectors.

In the late 1930s Imperial licensed the technology for making cheap pocketknives with hollow sheet-steel handles, covered with sheet celluloid, from inventors Ernst Löhr and Otto Stiehl of Solingen (Löhr's own knives were marked ELOSI). Imperial steadily improved this technology, receiving about a dozen patents in the next two decades. By 1940 Imperial was producing 100,000 of these "Jackmaster, HAMMER BRAND" knives per

**Schrade LB-7 folding hunter, custom scrimshaw deer head by Jim Gullette, Greer, South Carolina, 1979.**

**Schrade Cutlery Co., Walden, NY, four-blade senator penknife. Schrade "peach seed" jigged bone.**

**Schrade Cutlery Co., Walden, NY, Safety Push Button Knife, celluloid handles.**

day. After 1960 the trademark DIAMOND EDGE was applied to many of these knives.

In 1943 the Mirandos and Fazzano joined forces with Albert M. Baer of Ulster, and in 1946 they together took over Schrade Cutlery Co. The resulting Imperial Knife Associated Companies become the world's leading cutlery manufacturer.

## SCHRADE CUTLERY CO/G. SCHRADE/ SCHRADE-WALDEN/IMPERIAL-SCHRADE

George Schrade was one of the most prolific and influential inventors in American cutlery history. In 1892–93 he introduced his Press-Button knife. It was the first switchblade suited to mass-production methods, although automatic opening knives made by hand had been around for more than a century.

In 1903 George Schrade sold the rights to this knife, which has the release button in the front bolster, to Walden Knife Co, then owned by E. C. Simmons Hardware Co. The following year, he and his brothers Louis and William started their own Schrade Cutlery Co, also in Walden, New York. Besides a full line of conventional knives, they made Schrade Safety Push Button knives, with the release in the handle and, after 1906, with a sliding safety latch beside the button. More significantly, George Schrade invented and manufactured an array of automatic machines for making and assembling pocketknife components, which were widely adopted across the US, and in Britain, France, and Germany.

In 1925 George Schrade formed the George Schrade Knife Co in Bridgeport, Connecticut. Its ultra-modern knives, such as the patented "Wire-Jack", excite less collector interest today than the more traditional patterns made by Schrade Cutlery Co.

George Schrade died in 1945, and the following year his brothers sold Schrade Cutlery Co. to "Kingston" (Ulster and Imperial, see pages 38 and 39). The resulting Imperial Schrade Associated Companies adopted the brand name SCHRADE-WALDEN for its top line made in Schrade's old Walden, New York, plant. Schrade-Walden knives are more popular with collectors today than are the older ones from Schrade Cutlery (perhaps because they are more familiar).

In 1942 Albert M. Baer of Ulster had brought his brother,

Henry, into the firm. In the early 1950s Henry Baer became the president of the Schrade division, and Schrade's premium "Uncle Henry" line is named after him.

After World War II Imperial Knife Associated Companies both expanded and consolidated. At various times the firm owned major factories in France, Germany, and England (1977–1982). The Walden operation was closed in about 1973. In 1984 Fazzano and the Mirandos sold their interests to Albert M. Baer, and the firm became Imperial Schrade Corporation. All US pocket- and sport-knife production was consolidated in a new plant in Ellenville. Today all the "Jackmaster"-type knives are made in Listowel, Ireland.

Today Schrade offers a wide array of commemorative and limited edition knives for collectors. Best known is the annual "Schrade Scrimshaw" wildlife series, made since 1976.

## CAMILLUS CUTLERY CO
In 1894 Charles Sherwood built and operated a small pocketknife plant in Camillus, New York. From 1896 to 1898 he leased it to Millard Robeson. Then,

ABOVE

**Annual "Schrade Scrimshaw" wildlife limited edition set.**

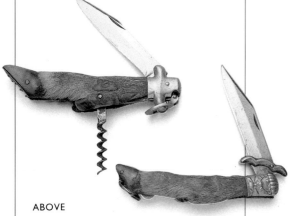

ABOVE

**Two A. W. Wadsworth & Sons, Austria, deerfoot folding knives, imported by Adolph Kastor & Bros., New York, from Bohemia prior to World War I.**

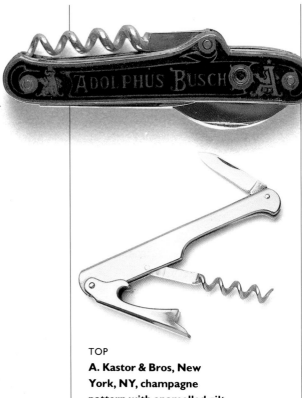

TOP

**A. Kastor & Bros, New York, NY,** champagne pattern with enamelled gilt brass handles, made for St Louis brewer Adolphus Busch (1839–1913), the man behind the international success of the Anheuser Busch Co. More than 60 varieties of fancy Busch knives are known. They were made for Busch personally, mainly by Kastor and by Wester Bros.

BOTTOM

**Camillus** waiter's knife, all metal.

ABOVE

**Camillus** recent small rope knife.

in 1902, it was purchased by Adolph Kastor, a leading New York City cutlery importer and wholesaler.

In 1922 Kastor hired 16-year-old Albert M. Baer as a stock clerk. Soon Baer went out on the road as a salesman, and quickly became the leading representative for Kastor and Camillus. Baer sold to retailers and jobbers in every state, but his main focus was to sell private brand knives to emerging mass-market retail chains. These included Sears Roebuck & Co (Sta-Sharp, Dunlap, and Kwik-Kut brands in the 1930s, Craftsman brand later – Tom Dunlap was the Sears hardware buyer who created the Craftsman hardware brand in 1926); F. W. Woolworth (Kent brand); and Kresge (now K-Mart). Baer even persuaded the baseball star Babe Ruth to endorse a Camillus pocketknife, a baseball bat figural, in 1930.

After the demise of New York Knife Co in 1931, Camillus became the leading US contract maker of private brand knives, a position the firm still enjoys today. Albert M. Baer left Kastor/Camillus in 1938, but retained a major stake in the firm, which is now a controlling interest owned by his children and grandchildren.

In the 1930s and 1940s Camillus was the leading US maker of character and figural pocketknives, many marked with its budget CAMCO brand. Other Camillus brands have included Catskill, Clover, Corning, Cornwall, Fairmount, Farragut, Federal, Mumbly Peg, Stainless Cutlery Co, Streamline, Sword Brand, and Syracuse Knife Co. Kastor/Camillus has also been a leading supplier of advertising knives, including many of the de luxe Anheuser Busch knives, and almost all of the genuine Coca-Cola knives.

Today Camillus makes many of the most popular limited edition collector knives, especially the reissue Remingtons. The firm also makes wildlife and other collector specials under its own name.

**UTICA – KUTMASTER/JACK KNIFE BEN** Though not as large nor as well known as some of its rivals, the Utica Cutlery Company of Utica, New York, has been an important American pocket cutlery firm since 1910. Utica has used many trademarks, including Agate Wood, American Maid, Featherweight, Iroquois, Seneca, and Pocket Pard, but by far its

TOP

**Camillus Cutlery Co, Camillus, NY, utility knife made for the US Army, World War II.**

BOTTOM

**Utica Cutlery Co, Utica, NY, Kutmaster brand utility knife made for the Medical Department, US Navy, World War II; used by Navy medics who served with the Marines.**

best-known brand is KUTMASTER, first adopted in 1937.

Utica has long been an active private brand contractor. Its two best-known contracts were with Chicago-based retailers. From the mid-1930s to the mid-1950s, Utica made WARDS brand pocketknives for Montgomery Ward, which were sold worldwide. From about 1927 until World War II, Utica made JACK KNIFE BEN knives for the popular and eccentric Benjamin W. Chon, whose Jack Knife Ben cutlery shop at the Chicago Stock Yards was, in its heyday (*circa* 1887 to the 1940s), a favourite tourist stop in the Windy City. Today JACK KNIFE BEN knives are much sought after by collectors. Some of the other firms that made Chon's knives before Utica were Napanoch (until 1919) and Schrade (until 1927).

Today Utica-Kutmaster specializes in making pocketknives with coined metal handles, both under its own name and on contract. For example, Utica makes the metal-handled Winchester reissues for Blue Grass Cutlery.

**BUCK KNIVES** The term "Buck Knife" is today virtually synonymous with Buck's Model 110 folding hunting knife. Yet the first Buck knives, made by Hoyt Heath Buck in Washington state early this century, were fixed blades. Indeed until 1962 all Buck knives were hand-made fixed blades, and fixed blades are still an important part of the Buck line.

In 1962, when Alfred and Charles Buck (son and grandson of H. H. Buck) were starting their first factory, Al Buck reasoned that some hunters might like a folding hunting knife which was stouter than any on the market. He did not expect it to be a big seller, but he felt that it would be a useful addition to the line.

As predicted, the new Buck 110 Folding Hunting knife did appeal to hunters. It also caught the eye of motorcyclists, construction workers, police officers, and ordinary citizens who liked the idea of a sturdy lock-back folding knife that they could carry in a compact belt sheath. The Model 110 has now sold millions and is the most successful new knife design of all time, as well as the most copied. Early versions of the Model 110 are now eagerly sought after by Buck collectors, as are the etched-blade limited edition knives which Buck has sold since the mid-1970s.

Buck also sells a range of other folding knives, both hunters

ABOVE
**Presentation boxed Gerber folding sportsman with engraved brass frame and green jade handle inlays.**

and pocket patterns. From 1966 to 1968, Buck's smaller knives were contract made by Schrade. From 1968 to about 1980, Camillus made those knives. Since then Buck has made all but one or two of the Buck patterns in its own plant, in El Cajon, California.

### GERBER LEGENDARY BLADES/AL MAR KNIVES/KERSHAW CUTLERY CO

Joseph R. Gerber, an advertising man in Portland, Oregon, designed the first Gerber knife (a carver) in 1939. Eventually Gerber opened a factory to make carving knives and steak knives, all with cast aluminium handles.

In the 1960s Gerber began to make hunting knives and combat survival knives, and in 1967 expanded the range to include the "Fh" model Folding Hunter, in three handle and two blade metal variations. The tool-steel chequered-walnut handle version is now much sought after by Japanese collectors.

Later the "Fh" was replaced by the metal-framed Folding Sportsman series of folding hunters. Gerber has its own wood shop, allowing it to offer cased presentation-quality knives, including Folding Sportsmen with handle inlays of semi-precious stones. In 1977 Gerber began to import a secondary line of smaller folding knives from Japan, sold under the name Silver Knight. From 1978 to 1986, Gerber made the patented Gerber-Paul button-lock folding knives, designed by Paul Poehlmann. These are now very much in demand among US collectors. Since 1986 Gerber has been owned by Fiskars, a cutlery firm in Helsinki, Finland, founded in 1649.

Two former Gerber employees have established their own cutlery companies in Oregon, both primarily importing knives from Japan. One is Pete Kershaw, who started Kershaw Cutlery in 1974. The other was Al Mar, who started Al Mar Knives in

# CUTLERY WHOLESALERS
· · · · · · · · · · · · · · · · · · · ·

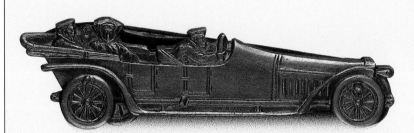

LEFT

**Germania Cutlery Works car figural knife, imported by Adolph Kastor & Bros, New York, NY.**

Specialized wholesale cutlery firms played almost as large a role in 19th-century American cutlery distribution as the wholesale hardware companies did. Most of those distribution firms were based in the cutlery district of lower Manhattan in New York City.

Before the Civil War there were dozens of firms, whose salesmen sold English, German, and American cutlery to retailers and hardware wholesalers across the United States. By the 1890s a few firms had become dominant, and the most notable are listed below.

In the decades since World War II, while regional hardware wholesaling faded away, specialized cutlery wholesaling has continued to prosper. Some wholesale firms promote their own private brands (such as Gutmann Cutlery's Explorer brand), but most distribute a variety of widely advertised manufacturers' brands.

**BOKER** The oldest American wholesale cutlery firm still in business is Hermann Boker & Co, established in 1837 by German immigrants in New York with branches in Canada and Mexico. Boker later built its own factories in Solingen and in New Jersey. The German branch is now the parent company.

**KASTOR** The largest American cutlery wholesaler was Adolph Kastor & Bros, founded in 1876. Its Germania Cutlery Works in Solingen (run by Nathan Kastor from 1885 to *c*1938) operated as a factor commissioning American-style cutlery to be made by Solingen craftsmen and factories. In 1902 Kastor bought and expanded the Camillus Cutlery Company as a source of tariff-free American-made knives. In addition to the many Camillus brands, Kastor trademarks included Clover (four leaves for the four Kastor brothers),

Imperial Razor Co, Cutwell, Germania, A. W. Wadsworth, W. H. Morley, J. Koester's Sons (the German spelling of Kastor), Duane Cutlery Co (named after Duane Street, lower Manhattan), Ebro and XLNT (both acquired in Sheffield), Pathfinder, and Big Chief. The Kastor name and most of these brands were last used in around 1947. Camillus Cutlery Co is now the firm's name, and it is closely associated with Imperial Schrade. It is strictly a manufacturer now, not a wholesaler.

**WIEBUSCH & HILGER** In 1864 William Hilger and Frederick Wiebusch, both with wholesale hardware experience, began their firm, which grew to be one of the most important. They bought factories in Sheffield (such as B. J. Eyre & Co in 1876), in Germany, and in Nixdorf, Bohemia (a major pocketknife centre before World War I). In 1891 they built the Challenge Cutlery Co in Bridgeport, Connecticut. Their brands included Atlantic, Western, Monumental, Walter Bros, Princeton, Owl, and Challenge. The firm closed in 1928 with the death of second-generation Charles F. Wiebusch. His extensive and unmatched knife collection is now in the Smithsonian Institution.

Other important wholesalers, some affiliated with particular factories, included the following. All were located in New York City, except as noted:

George Borgfeldt ● Butler Bros (Chicago IL) ● F. A. Clauberg & Co ● Coast Cutlery (Portland OR) ● J. Curley & Bros ● Graef & Schmidt (introduced J. A. Henckels to the US) ● J. S. Holler (represented by Adolph Blaich in San Francisco) ● R. J. Roberts ● Vom Cleff & Co ● Wester Bros (agents for Wester & Butz)

1979. Both firms sell knives around the world which are beginning to attract collector interest.

### ·········· HARDWARE WHOLESALERS ··········

Hardware wholesaler "house brands" are an up-and-coming specialty in pocketknife collecting. The evolution of hardware distribution was a key chapter in the historical development of North America, with the heyday of the wholesale hardware house lasting from about 1840 to 1940. Then every American and Canadian city of any size had at least two or three full-line wholesale hardware firms. Before 1800 there were very few; today there are even fewer.

The smallest served a radius of about fifty to a hundred miles (80 to 160 km). They supplied local hardware and general merchandise shops with a wide array of goods at several price points, on short notice, and usually on generous credit terms.

More typical hardware wholesalers served larger regions, encompassing several states. Beyond these, New York City, at first, and later San Francisco, Chicago, Saint Louis, Duluth, and Hamilton, Ontario, were home to giant hardware wholesale houses with nationwide and international distribution.

These firms allowed a large selection of merchandise to be offered to a population widely dispersed on millions of family farms and in thousands of small towns. The wholesalers gave local merchants the means to supply rural customers with the latest products enjoyed by their urban brethren.

The big wholesale firms grew up with a series of technological revolutions. After 1807 the steamboat and the railway after 1830, allowed salesmen and the goods which they sold to travel out to thousands of tiny local retailers in every corner of the continent. In 1844, the telegraph and the telephone after 1876 allowed these hardware and cutlery salesmen to stay on the road for months, but to send in their orders every day for immediate attention. Mass-production had first been introduced in 1798, but after 1865 it developed rapidly. The salesmen therefore had a large variety of standardized, inexpensive hardware and cutlery items to sell, and in the mid-1800s, it became possible to print illustrated hardware catalogues which kept on selling, even when the salesman was not around.

ABOVE
**Reprint of a 1925 Ka-Bar catalogue sheet. The "Grizzly" is a large, stag handled, clasp type switchblade.**

**PRIVATE BRANDS** By the 1870s, wholesale territories increasingly overlapped and competition grew intense. Hardware distributors began putting their own brand names on merchandise that they sold, especially cutlery, which was a profitable high-value line. In this way they could develop brand loyalty among both consumers and retailers.

By World War I there were dozens of private hardware house cutlery brands across the US and Canada. Most were local or regional, but some were better known nationwide than most manufacturers' brands, and those national hardware brands, especially KEEN KUTTER, are highly collectible today. Some collectors specialize in obscure brands, or in brands from their own city or region.

Some of the best-known pocketknife hardware brands are listed (see box).

This private brand pocket cutlery for the hardware houses was made by contract manufacturers in the US and Germany. Sheffield cutlery firms did much private brand work for American retailers before 1860 and a little between 1865 and 1890, but the US Tariff Act of 1891 virtually barred them from the American market. Thousands of Sheffield and Solingen cutlers emigrated to find work in the US.

The most important cutlery contractors before World War I were New York Knife Company and Ulster Knife Company, both

## HARDWARE BRANDS

• Keen Kutter, William Enders Oak Leaf, Chipaway, Hornet *(E. C. Simmons Hardware Co,* St Louis MO; branches at Philadelphia PA, Toledo OH, Sioux City IA, Minneapolis MN, Wichita KS) • Diamond Edge, Bridge *(Shapleigh Hardware Co,* St Louis MO. Owned Keen Kutter brand after 1940) • John Primble India Steel Works, Blue Grass, Pine Knot *(Belknap Hardware Co,* Louisville KY). [These brands are now owned by a small distributor called Blue Grass Cutlery Co in Manchester OH, which also sells the authorized Winchester reissues] • Our Very Best, True Value *(Hibbard, Spencer Bartlett & Co,* Chicago IL – now True Value Hardware Stores) • Zenith, Hartford *(Marshall Wells Hardware Co,* Duluth MN; branches at Portland OR, Spokane WA, Billings MT, Great Falls MT, and at Winnipeg MB, Edmonton AB, and Vancouver BC, Canada) • Henry Sears 1865 *(Farwell Ozmun Kirk & Co,* St Paul MN) • Stiletto, Damascus, Golden Gate *(Baker Hamilton & Pacific,* San Francisco CA; sales offices around the Pacific Rim) • Clean Cut, Springbrooke *(Dunham, Carrigan & Hayden,* San Francisco CA) • Red Devil *(Smith & Hemenway,* Utica NY).

ABOVE
**Shapleigh Hardware Co "Diamond-Edge" brand muskrat.**

ABOVE
**Remington UMC dog stripping knife, bone stag handles.**

in upstate New York, and both of which were started and largely staffed by Sheffield emigrants. Other important early contractors were Connecticut firms Waterville, Empire, Southington, and Challenge; New Jersey's Boker/Valley Forge; Western States of Colorado; and New York state's Schrade, Union, Napanoch, and Walden (the latter two absorbed by Winchester in 1919 and 1923). Leading early German contractors were Wester & Butz, Gebruder Weyersberg, and P. Daniel Peres.

Since 1922 the dominant American private brand pocketknife contractor has been Camillus. Other leading contemporary pocketknife contractors are Queen, Utica, and Alcas (maker of Cutco household knives).

### REMINGTON TRANSFORMS THE HARDWARE BUSINESS
In 1919 Remington Arms entered the pocketknife business, and within five years had become the dominant American manufacturer. Remington did no private brand work, but pioneered high-profile worldwide marketing of their own Remington UMC brand, now one of the most collectible. Hardware houses in every state and nation jumped on this bandwagon, most abandoning their house brands in favour of the pre-sold Remington line.

The Depression of 1929 to 1940 weeded out the weaker and less flexible hardware houses, the ones which were under-capitalized, or which failed to adapt to changing times. It also bankrupted Remington, which had extended credit to all of the houses, but the DuPont company took over and saved Remington in 1933.

What really killed the wholesale hardware business was World War II – four long years of virtually no business for any of the houses. And Remington, which had become their mainstay knife line, had abruptly dropped out of the cutlery business in 1940, leaving a vacuum which no other knife firm was able to fill.

Even the strong hardware firms which did survive the war found the world transformed after 1945. Diversity and high quality had nearly vanished from cutlery manufacture; markets were flooded with military surplus knives; once-famous brand names had been forgotten by the fickle public; and population was concentrating in big cities and their suburbs. A few hardware houses adapted by developing suburban retailer networks,

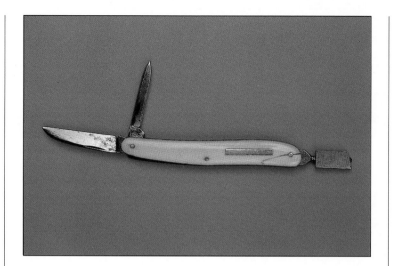

following the "Winchester Store" model that had been pioneered – prematurely, as it turned out – by Winchester-Simmons in the 1920s. Today "True Value" is the best known of these retailer networks, but it does not sell private brand knives. Most of the great old hardware wholesalers quietly faded away.

#### ···· SHEFFIELD AND THE UNITED STATES ·····

From the time of American independence, declared in 1776, up until 1891, the fortunes of Sheffield and of the United States were closely intertwined. Sheffield was, for the US, the source of most of its higher-quality cutlery; of nearly all of its blade, spring, and tool steel; of much of its steel-making technology and capital; and of a large share of its citizens working in the cutlery and steel trades. To Sheffield, America was its largest export market by far, as well as the new home of thousands of its sons and daughters.

### THE GIANTS: JOSEPH RODGERS AND GEORGE WOSTENHOLM

**JOSEPH RODGERS & SONS** Joseph Rodgers & Sons of Sheffield was, in the 19th century, the best-known brand of cutlery in the world. Indeed Rodgers cutlery, with its Star-Cross trademark, was probably the first brand-name product to be familiar to people all around the globe. In the remotest mountain village or island jungle, the word "Rodgers" became synonymous with the local word for "best".

A member of the Rodgers family was granted the trademark of a six-point star and Maltese cross in 1682. Joseph and Maurice Rodgers brought the firm to national prominence in the 18th

LEFT
**Wade & Butcher, Sheffield, England, race knife (timber scriber) with auxiliary sheepfoot blade, bone stag handles.**

## SHEFFIELD

A list of Sheffield cutlers and cutlery firms whose knives were sold in the United States would fill an entire book. Here are the names of some of the more prominent (courtesy Geoffrey Tweedale):

Joseph Rodgers & Sons ● George Wostenholm & Son ● Naylor & Sanderson ● John Sorby & Sons ● Marsh Brothers ● William Greaves & Sons ● Benjamin James Eyre & Co ● Frederick Ward & Co ● William & Samuel Butcher (Wade & Butcher) ● Thomas Turner & Company ● (Wade) Wingfield, Rowbotham & Co ● Joseph Haywood ● William Gilchrist ● Wilson, Hawksworth & Moss (& Ellison) ● Mappin Brothers ● Henry Barge ● John Hinchcliffe ● Unwin & Rodgers ● Richard Bunting ● Jonathan Crookes & Son ● Sleigh Rowland ● Luke Booth ● Henry C. Booth ● Samuel Wragg & Sons ● George Woodhead ● John Askham ● Broomhead & Thomas ● James Westa ● John Coe ● Brookes & Crookes ● Harrison Brothers & Howson ● Herbert M. Slater ● Charles Ibbotson ● George Hides & Son ● Champion & Co ● Michael Hunter & Son ● George Ibberson & Co

ABOVE
**Knife by Samuel C. Wragg, Sheffield, England (c1830s–1860s).**

century as makers of high-quality pocketknives and razors, but its worldwide fame was largely the work of John Rodgers (1779–1859).

John Rodgers expanded the firm's product line to include the complete range of cutlery. In the 1820s he won a Royal Warrant, allowing the firm to add the Royal Cypher to its mark. A member of the Rodgers firm maintained a permanent office in New York to foster the US trade, a decisive factor in the expansion of the firm's Norfolk Street Works into the world's largest cutlery factory by 1850.

Like the rest of Sheffield, Rodgers was hurt by the steep tariffs which were introduced by the United States in 1891 and increased in 1901 and after. Yet more than any of its Sheffield rivals, Rodgers had other markets to fall back upon. Its cutlery was the best-known brand throughout the British Empire and far beyond the empire's borders.

**GEORGE WOSTENHOLM & SON – I\*XL** George Wolstenholme began the manufacture of cutlery near Sheffield in 1745. Before 1815, his grandson, George, who shortened the family name to Wostenholm, occupied a workshop in Sheffield called the Rockingham Works. This George's son, also George, was born in 1800. He joined the family firm before 1824 and in 1826 registered the trademark I\*XL ("I excel").

Keenly aware of the growing American market, the Wostenholms in 1830 made a consignment of cutlery to William Stenton, who travelled for Naylor & Sanderson, a leading factor and exporter to the US. This venture proved so successful that the

Wostenholms thereafter devoted all of their efforts to making
cutlery for the US market. In 1848 the younger Wostenholm,
whose father had died in 1833, moved the firm into the
Washington Works, a very large and modern factory. Befitting its
name, all the cutlery made there was sold in the United States.
Asline Ward ran the firm's New York sales office, but George
Wostnholm himself made thirty sales trips across the Atlantic
during his lifetime.

Within a few years Wostenholm's I*XL had become the best-
known and best-selling brand of cutlery in the U.S. American
hardware and cutlery merchants, whatever other brands they sold
or distributed, always carried a good selection of I*XL
pocketknives, bowie knives, and razors. George Wostenholm
died in 1876, one of the wealthiest men in Yorkshire.

The American "protective" tariffs of 1891 and after devastated
G. Wostenholm & Son. The US was its only market, and the firm
lost 90 per cent of its American trade almost overnight. For
another nine decades US retailers continued to carry a token
selection of I*XL knives (over-priced for their quality, because of
the tariff), so powerful was the goodwill built up for the mark by
George Wostenholm. Belatedly the firm sought customers in other
lands, but rival firms (especially Rodgers) were there already,
and no other market was as lucrative as the US. Wostenholm's
best 20th-century market proved to be Canada, where the great
Hudson's Bay Company became its leading outlet.

**RODGERS-WOSTENHOLM/RICHARDS/SCHRADE I*XL**  Both Rodgers
and Wostenholm enjoyed modest prosperity after World War I.
Then in 1971, the two long-time Sheffield rivals merged. In 1975,
the combined firm was absorbed by Richards Bros, scion of the
German Richartz firm, and British licensee of the Löhr and Stiehl
patents for cheap mass-produced pocketknives.

In 1977 Richards was purchased by Albert M. Baer of
Imperial-Schrade. He moved Rodgers-Wostenholm into
Richards' Morse Street factory, built by Wilhelm Muller in 1946,
the largest and most modern plant in Sheffield. From there came
the SCHRADE-I*XL pocketknives, actively marketed to
American collectors. This acquisition was a money-loser,
however, so Baer sold the plant in August 1982. Four months
later it was in receivership, and a year and a half after that it was

ABOVE
**I*XL George Wostenholm,
sailor's knife marked U.S.
NAVY, genuine stag handle.**

ABOVE
**I*XL George Wostenholm,
Sheffield, four-blade shadow
senator, genuine stag
handles.**

ABOVE
**George Wostenholm & Son, I\*XL horseman's combination knife with genuine stag handles. Blades (clockwise from top left): fleam (for bleeding foundered horses), saw, spear master blade, pen blade, hoof-pick/nut-cracker, gimlet, awl, corkscrew; pick and tweezers in handles.**

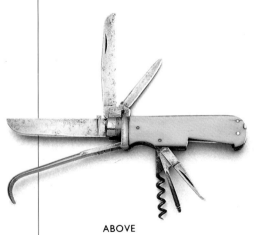

ABOVE
**G. Smith & Sons, Sheffield, horseman's knife, ivory handles; integral bolster-liners and narrow square kicks indicate a knife made in Sheffield prior to c1860.**

torn down. The Rodgers and Wostenholm trademarks (and many other old Sheffield names) are now owned by a small manufacturing firm in Sheffield called the Egginton Group, which makes pocketknives and other cutlery for sale in Britain.

**OTHER LEADING SHEFFIELD FIRMS** While Rodgers and Wostenholm were the English cutlery firms best known outside Britain, other cutlery firms in Sheffield were equally well known in the British Isles, and grew large and prosperous in the 19th century.

● **Thomas Turner & Company** was founded in 1802, and by the 1820s was located in Norfolk Street. In around 1834 the firm opened its Suffolk Works to make cutlery, tools, and crucible steel. By 1905 Turner's employed roughly 1,000 men. The firm went out of business in 1932.

● **Mappin Brothers**, which began as the engraving firm of Joseph Mappin in 1810, began to make cutlery in about 1820. In 1851 the firm moved to the Queen's Cutlery Works, where its labour force grew to over 200 in the next decade. Multi-blade sportsman's knives were a speciality, but the firm offered several thousand pocketknife patterns. In 1902 Mappin Bros was absorbed by an allied firm, MAPPIN & WEBB. Thereafter the combined firm increasingly specialized in plated wares, and more recently in jewellery.

● **Unwin & Rodgers** (c1828–1867) was best known for its "patented pistol-knife".

● **Jonathan Crookes & Son** (Heart and Pistol brand) was founded in 1780. This firm enjoyed a high reputation on both sides of the Atlantic.

● **Brookes & Crookes** (Atlantic Works) were founded in 1858 by Thomas Crookes and John Brookes. The firm employed over 150 workers by the 1890s, and specialized in elaborate sportsman's and ladies' knives.

● **Harrison Brothers & Howson** enjoyed royal patronage almost from its foundation in 1796 by William Sansom. The firm was acquired in 1847 by James W. Harrison, William Howson, and Henry Harrison. The latter opened American agencies in New York and San Francisco. By 1896 the company employed over 700. Its Alpha Works remained open until 1963.
over 700. Its Alpha Works endured until 1963.

- **George Ibberson & Co's** Violin brand pocketknives earned high esteem. This brand was registered in 1880, but the Ibberson family had been prominent in Sheffield cutlery making since 1666. In 1914 Joseph Ibberson was selected to harden and grind the first stainless steel knife blades in history. The firm closed its doors in 1988.
- **George Butler & Co's** Trinity Works were founded in 1768. Though still in business, Butler's last made pocketknives in 1972. Butler trademarks included "Cavendish" (after a noble patron), "Art", and a picture of a key. The firm sold its knives principally in Britain, and in Australia, India, and the other colonies. It enjoyed royal patronage, making among other splendid things a 600-piece ivory-handled cutlery set for the Prince of Wales in 1883.

················· SOLINGEN CUTLERY ·················

Since the late Middle Ages, Solingen, Germany, has been a centre of steel and blade manufacture. Through much of its early history, Solingen was dependent on older and larger Cologne. By the 18th century Solingen blades had earned their own high reputation, but a rigid guild structure limited production of Solingen cutlery for European and world markets.

The first break in this system was made by Peter Daniel Peres, who became a cutlery merchant in 1792 at the age of 16. In 1805 the ruler of Solingen, Duke Maximilian of Bavaria, granted Peres a charter to erect Solingen's first water-powered pocketknife factory.

Soon after, Maximilian traded Solingen to Emperor Napoleon Bonaparte of France. Napoleon abolished all the privileges and monopolies of the Solingen guilds, clearing the way for the rapid development of the city's sword and cutlery industry. In 1815 Solingen became part of the Kingdom of Prussia. Many large and well-known cutlery factories were established there in the next half-century, although the majority were "factories" in the old sense: the warehouses of factors. Most Solingen cutlery was still made by outworkers in their home workshops.

Solingen's cutlery factors and merchants actively sought export markets around the world. Many of them set up sales branches or export agencies in the United States. Solingen cutlery was so competitively priced that even the US protective tariffs after 1891

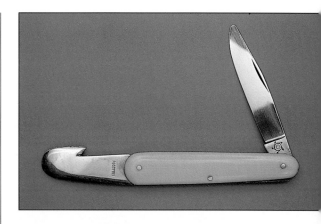

TOP
**Bone handled folding citrus knife by Mueller & Schmidt, Pfeilringwerk (Arrow Circle Works), Solingen.**
BOTTOM
**H. Kaufmann & Sons, Solingen, spirit level knife.**

ABOVE
**Boker, 2¾ in (7 cm), all metal handles, etched Girl Scout emblem on handle, one blade.**

ABOVE
**W. R. Case & Sons plier knife, contract made by Boker/Valley Forge (1923 Charles Undy patent), bone handles.**

did little to keep it out of the American market. By 1900 Solingen's cutlery exports exceeded those of Britain, France, and the United States combined. Virtually every American hardware and cutlery wholesaler offered a selection of low-cost knives made in Solingen. A few of them also offered top-quality Solingen knives, but at that time "Made in Germany" was pretty much synonymous with cheap price and low quality.

World War I closed world markets to German cutlery from 1915 until the early 1920s, by which time American firms had come to dominate the cutlery industry, both high quality and low. Four-fifths of the Solingen export trade was lost, and many of the city's cutlery firms failed. Aerial bombardment in World War II destroyed more of the Solingen cutlery industry, and although that industry is still healthy today, it is but a shadow of its former self, eclipsed by both Japan and the United States.

**H. BOKER & CO/VALLEY FORGE** In 1837 Hermann and Robert Boker, two brothers who had been partners in the sword-making business near Solingen since 1829, emigrated to North America. Hermann started H. Boker & Co in New York City, importing cutlery, tools, and steel from Germany and England. Robert went to Canada and then to Mexico City, where he founded Casa Roberto Boker. Hermann moved his warehouse to Newark, New Jersey, but retained the H. Boker & Co office in Manhattan.

In 1869 their cousin, Heinrich Boker, with a cutler named Hermann Heuser, opened a factory in Solingen to manufacture "Tree Brand" pocketknives and other cutlery for both H. Boker and Casa R. Boker to sell. Their trademark, TREE BRAND, had long been used by the family's tool works in Remschied. Besides this German cutlery, H. Boker & Co also imported Sheffield cutlery under a variety of house brands, including Manhattan Cutlery Co and John Newton & Co.

Like other importers responding to the US Tariff Act of 1891, H. Boker & Co sought domestic sources of high-quality pocket cutlery. In 1899 Boker bought the Valley Forge Cutlery Co in Newark (founded in 1892). Both Valley Forge and Boker brand knives were made there, plus many private brands for other distributors, and for advertising speciality firms such as Newark's Whitehead & Hoag (knives marked THE W. & H. CO.).

After World War I Boker sold its Newark plants and built a new factory complex in Maplewood, New Jersey. The Valley

Forge brand was last used in about 1950. Boker briefly owned the George Schrade Knife Co, from 1956 to 1958, but closed it when the manufacture of switchblade knives for interstate sale was banned in the US in 1958.

In 1969 the J. Wiss & Sons scissors firm (established in Newark in 1847) acquired H. Boker & Co. In 1978, Wiss sold Boker to the Cooper Tool Group of North Carolina. Cooper closed the Maplewood plant in 1984 and ceased making cutlery.

In 1986 Cooper sold US rights in all Boker trademarks to Heinrich Boker & Co of Solingen. Boker's American sales office is now in Golden, Colorado. Under the direction of its president, Chuck Hoffman, Boker USA now sells an up-to-date range of German pocket cutlery, including de luxe special editions with blades of damascus steel, and even of ceramic. H. Boker of Solingen is also a leading private brand contractor.

**J. A. Henckels – Twinworks** Johann Peter Henckels began making table cutlery in Solingen on 13 June, 1731. His trademark was a conjoined pair of twins. The Henckels firm was inherited by Johann Abraham Henckels the Elder late in the 18th century, and by his son, J. A. Henckels the Younger, in around 1836. In 1840 Henckels acquired its present *Zwillingswerk* (Twinworks) factory. It was the first Solingen firm to use steam power, and one of the first to make its own blade steel.

In the mid-19th century, Henckels sought export markets for its cutlery throughout Europe. The company owned showrooms in Berlin, Cologne, Dresden, Munich, Vienna, and Paris, and exhibited at Worlds Fairs in England, France, and the US.

In 1883 Henckels began to export a full range of cutlery to the United States, through the agency of New York wholesaler Graef & Schmidt. From the beginning, Twin cutlery competed in America on quality, not on price. Different assortments of pocketknives were offered in each country, until the total number of patterns exceeded 2,000. About a quarter were sold in the US. From 1906 into the 1930s, Henckels master sales catalogues had all text printed in German, English, French, and Spanish.

The factory suffered bomb damage in 1944, but resumed business in 1947 with a drastically reduced selection. A small assortment of pocketknives was offered until 1960. Since then Henckels has occasionally offered pocketknives that carry its name and the Twins logo, and made by a variety of contractors.

ABOVE
**Boker "Tree Brand" muskrat.**

## SOLINGEN
· · · · · · ·

These are some of the important Solingen cutlery firms whose pocketknives are now of interest to collectors, with their starting dates (information courtesy Siegfried Rosenkaimer):

Gottlieb Hammesfahr (1684) ● Friedrich Herder Abr. Sohn (1727) ● J. A. Henckels (1731) ● Lauterjung & Son Pumawerk (1769) ● Carl Schlieper (1769) ● Gebruder Weyersberg (1787) ● Peter Daniel Peres (1792) ● David Everts (1806) ● Peter Daniel Baus (1820) ● Alexander Coppel (1821) ● Gebruder Christians (1824) ● Eduard Wusthof (1832) ● Robert Klaas (1834) ● C. Lutters & Co (1840) ● Carl & Robert Linder (1842) ● Gebruder Krusius (1856) ● C. Bertram (1864) ● Wilhelm Weltersbach (1882) ● Anton Wingen (1888) ● Ernst Brueckmann (1891) ● Friedrich Olbertz (1915) ● Hubertus (1932).

ABOVE
**Victorinox Super Timer and
Classic and tie-pin.**

·················· SWISS CUTLERY ··················

**VICTORINOX/WENGER** Victorinox and Wenger are rival firms in
Switzerland, both of which make pocketknives for the Swiss
Army, and both of which sell red-handled "Swiss Army" knives.

Victorinox, in Ibach, is the older firm. It was founded in 1884
by Karl Elsener, and his descendants own the firm today. His
mother's name was Victoria; *inoxydable* is French for "stainless"
Hence the firm's trademark: Victor(ia) + Inox(ydable)
= Victorinox. The Wenger firm, established in about 1908, is
located in Delemont.

Both firms make officer's and soldier's knives for the Swiss
Army. The original officer's model of 1897, prototype of all the
commercial versions, was a six-blade utility knife with red fibre
handles. The soldier's model, from 1891 until about 1960, was a
three-blade knife with bolsters at one end. The spear blade and
screwdriver were at that end, the tin-opener at the other. These
knives had wooden handles until 1908, then red fibre handles.
Often the blade is marked with the last two digits of the year of
issue. Since 1961 the soldier's knife has had aluminium handles
(coloured red until 1965).

Older Victorinox and Wenger knives are beginning to attract
collector attention. Also of potential interest are the firms'
advertising knives with metal handle inlays.

## V

CHAPTER

# FANCY HANDLES

## FIGURAL, ADVERTISING, CHARACTER, COMMEMORATIVE, SOUVENIR, AND LIMITED EDITION POCKETKNIVES

I n most pocketknives the important part is the blade or blades. The blades are the business end, the parts that do the work.

There is a class of pocketknife, however, whose principal work is communication rather than cutting. The shape, artwork, and inscriptions on the handles are more important than the blades.

Within this group of pocketknives, the handles do the real work:

● FIGURAL KNIVES are the oldest type. The majority of surviving Ancient Roman pocketknives are figural knives whose handles are miniature sculptures of people, parts of the human body (especially legs), animals, or objects.

● ADVERTISING KNIVES are usually given by business firms as mementos or presents to remind clients and potential customers about the firm whose name or trademark appears on the handle.

● CHARACTER AND CELEBRITY KNIVES depict popular fictional or fantasy characters, or real-life popular heroes. I have seen 1880s' pocketknives with cast pewter handles depicting characters from Gilbert and Sullivan operettas, but the heyday of character pocketknives was from the late 1930s until the early 1960s.

TOP
**Ambassador (Colonial Knife Co, Providence, RI) miniature keyring knife advertising Greencastle Livestock Market, Greencastle, Pa, "cracked ice" (imitation pearl) celluloid handles.**

BOTTOM
**Camco (Camillus) "Dick Tracy and Junior" character knife with magnifying glass and whistle.**

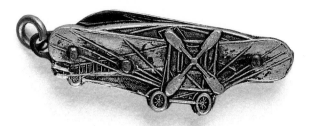

RIGHT
**Unmarked aeroplane figural knife.**

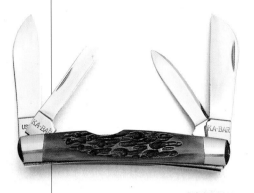

TOP
**Ka-Bar limited edition congress knife, red bone stag handles.**

MIDDLE
**Ambassador (Colonial Knife Co, Providence, RI) coin type knife, advertising Bethlehem, Pa, Chamber of Commerce.**

BOTTOM
**Hickock Mfg Co, Rochester, NY (men's jewellery manufacturer), "KoiNife", souvenir of Smith Corona 1940 Rodeo, silver handles.**

The names and faces of political figures began to appear on American pocketknives and razors early in the 19th century. The use of pocketknives in political campaigns continues to this day.

Perhaps the first entertainment celebrity to endorse the use of his likeness on a pocketknife was William F. "Buffalo Bill" Cody, whose Wild West show delighted big-city audiences on both sides of the Atlantic.

Photographs of sports heroes have adorned pocketknife handles since 1910. The first sports star to make an actual endorsement deal for a pocketknife was legendary baseball player Babe Ruth, in 1930. He received a royalty for allowing his autograph to be reproduced on a baseball bat figural knife.

● COMMEMORATIVE KNIVES, inspired by commemorative stamps and coins, record important anniversaries, either public or private. The oldest that I have seen, commemorating the Battle of Gettysburg, date from 1910, but this type of knife did not become commonplace until the rapid growth of knife collecting after 1970.

● SOUVENIR KNIVES, bought as souvenirs in the location where they were made, are an old tradition. American visitors to Sheffield bought knives as mementos in the 1830s, while visitors to San Francisco in the 1870s bought knives made there by Michael Price or Will & Finck. However knives made and explicity marked as souvenirs date back little more than a century. Generally they are inexpensive and designed to appeal to the mass market.

● LIMITED-EDITION KNIVES are those made expressly as collector items. Sometimes they are replicas of antique knives, and some are unofficial "commemoratives". Their quality ranges from shoddy to very fine, with the latter always a better bargain than the former, regardless of price.

Of special interest are the limited-edition knife club knives commissioned by local or regional collector clubs and offered for

**ABOVE**
**Selection of Schrade
commemorative knives
including (clockwise from
top left): Schrade Cutlery
85th anniversary, 1989;
Federal duck stamp, 1990/
1991; US National Park
Service 75th anniversary,
1991; 50th anniversary of
US entry into World War II,
1991.**

sale to their members. There are now knife clubs in many places, and they all welcome distant members who join by mail (see the list in *Knife World* magazine). Some clubs sponsor knife shows, which draw hundreds of exhibitors and thousands of visitors.

············ TYPES OF CONSTRUCTION ············

The subject matter and the production technology of fancy handled knives has evolved over the years. These knives were usually intended for mass-market sale, or to be given as free gifts, so low cost was usually a prime consideration. Technological innovations often appeared in advertising and souvenir knife construction long before they were applied to ordinary pocketknives.

The list below is a roughly chronological account of the types of handle construction used on fancy knives, along with comments on their application and significance.

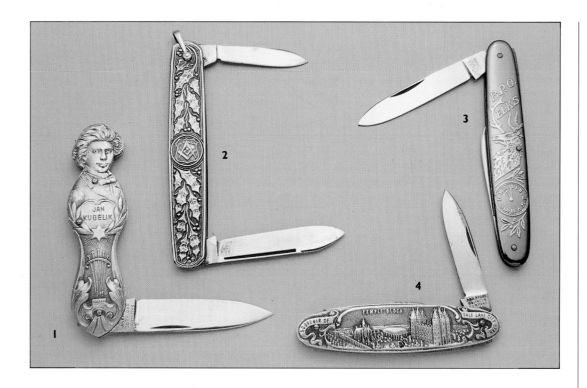

● **PRESSED HORN HANDLES.** Low-relief scenes pressed into horn handles, using steel dies and steam pressure, were perhaps the first mass-produced illustrated handles. Widely used in Sheffield in the late-18th and early-19th centuries, they were substantially cheaper to make than earlier figural knives, which were individually hand-carved. Individual hand-carving of figural boxwood handles persisted in Bohemia until World War I.

● **ENGRAVED IVORY, PEARL, OR BONE HANDLES.** Most of this work, which was still being crafted in the 1930s, was done by hand. Therefore it is found only on high-quality advertising knives given to important executives, rather than to ordinary consumers.

● **CAST OR COINED METAL HANDLES.** This technology was rapidly developed in the first year or two of the American Civil War (1860–1865). The typical cheap soldier's jack knife of that period had stamped brass or cast iron handles, often advertising the firm that made the knife. In the 1870s and 1880s James D. Frary of Bridgeport, Connecticut, made a large business of cheap pictorial pocketknives with cast pewter handles. In 1886 after aluminium had become available commercially, the Solingen firm of P. Daniel Peres made a speciality of commemorative, souvenir, advertising, and political pocketknives with highly detailed aluminium handles stamped in deep relief. Thereafter

many firms in Germany, France, and the US offered an endless variety of embossed handles in a variety of metals. Beware that most such knives with unplated *brass* handles are modern replicas or counterfeits.

● **MOULDED CELLULOID OR COMPOSITION HANDLES.** The invention of celluloid by J. W. Hyatt in 1869, and then of other plastics, allowed a renaissance of figural knives. With mouldable plastics for handles, these little sculptures could be mass-produced, rather than laboriously hand-carved.

● **CLEAR CELLULOID PICTURE HANDLES.** Celluloid could be made in a rainbow of colours and a world of patterns, but it could also be transparent. In 1879 Reuben and Henry Landis of Canton, Ohio, patented a method of bonding photographs or other pictures to clear celluloid to make durable picture-handled pocketknives. From this grew a large and important segment of the American pocket-cutlery industry of the "Golden Age". These picture knives could be bought with stock designs or illustrations, while advertisers or political candidates could order large quantities of custom-made knives.

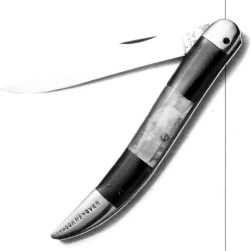

ABOVE
**Made in U.S.A. tickler with "loud" photo under clear celluloid handle.**

Most appealing to the public, however, was the service offered by such firms as Novelty Cutlery Co, Canton Cutlery Co, Aerial Cutlery Co, Golden Rule Cutlery Co, and a handful of others. These firms would assemble a knife to order for a retail customer, using text and photos supplied by that customer through a local representative, and do so at a price competitive with plain pocketknives of comparable quality. Such "custom" pocketknives sold by the millions from the 1880s up to the 1930s,

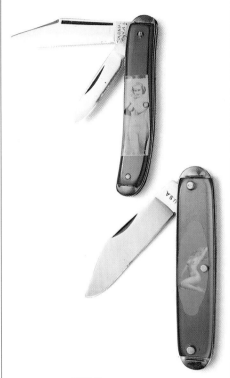

ABOVE
**Two Colonial jack knives
with "loud" photographs
under clear plastic handles.
Top (black and white) is
original c1950. Bottom
(colour, of Marilyn Monroe),
is recent.**

RIGHT
**Imperial equal-end jack,
enamelled handles, souvenir
of New York World's Fair,
1964–1965.**

and are today a popular collecting speciality. In recent years there has been a small-scale revival of the "picture handle", using clear plastic over lithographed images.

● ENAMELLED METAL HANDLES. Cloisonné-like enamel-handled pocketknives were developed in Solingen around 1890. Their ornate gilt brass frames were filled with multi-coloured enamels, making a gorgeous effect. Often these knives, as well as some with engraved pearl or ivory handles, incorporated tiny Stanhope lens "peepholes", containing miniature photographs (sometimes for advertising, sometimes risqué). These knives were very expensive, and their principal consumer was the American brewer, Adolphus Busch, who liked to give them away to people he met on his extensive world travels.

● COLOUR-ETCHED METAL HANDLES. Techniques combining etching with enamelling and selective electroplating, developed in Sweden and Germany early in the 20th century, were used to produce a wide variety of pocketknife handles with colourful, attractive, inexpensive, and relatively durable pictures, designs, and advertising messages. These knives are not yet appreciated by collectors as much as they deserve to be.

● STAMPED OR LITHOGRAPHED CELLULOID AND PLASTIC HANDLES. These simplest of techniques for decorating handles have been around for over a century, and are today the most widely used. They can vary from a spartan single line of type to elaborate full-colour and full-coverage illustrations.

● METAL INLAID CELLULOID OR PLASTIC HANDLES. The technique of moulding silhouettes or words cut from thin sheets of nickel silver into white or imitation pearl celluloid pocketknife handles was developed in Germany in around 1930. Today this technique is used on Swiss pocketknives with solid colour plastic handles.

# CHAPTER VI

# HAND CRAFTED FOLDING KNIVES

**P**rice-tag shock: that momentary feeling of dizziness one gets upon reading the price label on a new car, especially if one has not visited a dealer in several years.

If you have only seen pocketknives for sale in hardware, cutlery, or sporting-goods shops, you are likely to experience "price-tag shock" the first time you see hand-made pocketknives offered for sale at a knife show or in an art gallery or jewellery shop. As a rule of thumb, the price of a serviceable hand-made folding knife by a not-very-prominent knifemaker is ten times the price of a factory pocketknife of similar size. A comparable folding knife by a world-renowned maker might cost a further ten times more. To understand this phenomenon, it helps to have some historical perspective on hand-made folding knives.

#### ················· THE GOLDEN AGE ·················

The half century between 1890 and 1940 was the Golden Age of the American pocketknife. Beginning in the 1890s, "protective" tariffs curtailed the access of foreign cutlery firms to the American market. The American firms that had lobbied for higher duties then moved in aggressively to fill the gap. Not only

ABOVE
**"Falconer of the Maghreb".
Folding knife by Steve Hoel,
3¼ in (8.2cm) long when
closed. Inlaid with gold and
engraved by Jon Robyn.**

TOP
**"Golden Carp (Koi)". Folding knife by Tim Herman, 3½ in (8.9cm) long closed. Green jade handle inlays. Gold inlaid and engraved by D. Wilkerson.**

BOTTOM
**"Gentleman's Folding Knife" by Ron Lake. Total length when open, 4½ in (11.4cm). 18-carat gold frame and bail, pearl handle inlays.**

did they take over the US market from their English and German rivals, they also recruited some of the most talented Sheffield and Solingen pocket cutlers.

Thus reborn, the American pocketknife industry of that Golden Age was a conjoining of the best of old-world hand craftsmanship with the best of American industrial organization, marketing, and innovation. The result, for the American pocketknife buyer, was a rich bounty of wonderful folding knives. This development was interrupted briefly by World War I, but by 1920 it was back on track.

Before 1940 the best factory folding knives were in fact hand-made, their designs endlessly varied, their materials the best that science and nature could provide. Back then only a few makers, such as William Scagel and A. C. Cornelison did make small numbers of "indestructible" folding knives by hand.

### · · · · · · · · · · · · · · · · · · THE DARK AGE · · · · · · · · · · · · · · · · · ·

After World War II, however, the story was different. Many of the important pre-war pocketknife manufacturers had left the business, and most of the remaining pocket cutlery firms had experienced four years of the low standards, limited varieties, and guaranteed profits of war contracts.

During the war, however, while what remained of the cutlery industry was cranking out millions of "adequate" knives, hundreds of individual knifemakers, in and out of uniform, found the opportunity to hand-make thousands of better-than-ordinary knives, almost exclusively fixed blades. After the war, demand for hand-made knives declined.

### · · · · · · · · · · · · · · · THE RENAISSANCE · · · · · · · · · · · · · · · ·

The first serious move by an American hand knifemaker into folding knives was Al Buck's innovative Model 110 Folding Hunter of 1962. Buck never dreamed that this design would revolutionize the very idea of the folding knife, but it did, and it opened up a whole new world of markets, both to factory makers, whose ranks Buck was just joining, and to other hand knifemakers.

In the early 1970s a few new makers – including Ron Lake, Bob Hayes, Jess Horn, Jimmy Lile, Paul Poehlmann, Barry Wood, and Robert Ogg – struggled up onto the high ground abandoned by the folding-knife factories and made a solid start which earned them a growing customer following.

Two decades ago, "hand-made knife" was virtually synonymous with "fixed-blade knife". Today, by contrast, hand knifemakers increasingly face two choices: make folding knives, or starve. There is still some interest in hand-made fixed blades of the very best quality, but most of today's interest in hand-made knives, especially among collectors, is strictly in folding knives.

## ········· LOOKING AT FOLDING KNIVES ··········

The most important consideration in hand-made folding knives is workmanship: engineering design, materials selection, and the fundamentals of fit and finish. The baseline standard of workmanship – a very high standard – is set by today's factory folding knives. Many hand knifemakers cannot even equal that standard, let alone surpass it, so the fact that someone made a knife by hand does not necessarily mean that the knife is worth its price – or any price. By contrast, the very best hand-made folding knives are as well made as the finest Swiss watches, which explains why they are priced in the same range.

Very few top folding-knife makers do truly "custom" work to customer designs. Some customers have their knives "customized" with fine engraving and/or scrimshaw, but even the most amazing engraving does not enhance resale value *on the knife collector market*. In the knife-as-jewellery market, however, superb engraving is almost obligatory.

Some hand knifemakers sell directly to customers, but the best way to maximize selection and minimize delay is to buy through dealers who specialize in hand-made knives.

## ·········· FASHIONS IN FOLDING KNIVES ·········

Knife collecting is governed by fashions and fads. This is especially true in the collecting of contemporary hand-made knives, because knifemakers can, and do, invent new fashions.

A couple of years ago the hottest area in folding knives was innovative blade-locking mechanisms. New ones were shown at every knife show. Some were silly, some baffling, and some were very slick. Today there is still some interest in novel locks, but the most recent trend is simplicity of line and flawless execution.

Another popular area is damascus steel folding knives. Most damascus is built up of multiple layers of steel, iron, and

## TODAY'S TOP FOLDER MAKERS
· · · · · · · · · · · · · · ·

Here is a list of the very best and most popular (and most expensive) folding-knife makers working today. Expect to pay $1,000 (£600) – or a great deal more – for one of their knives.

Apart from this select few, there is a larger group of several dozen extremely good folding-knife makers, men and women whose work certainly surpasses factory standards. Some of them will undoubtedly join the top rank, as they refine their skills or become better known.

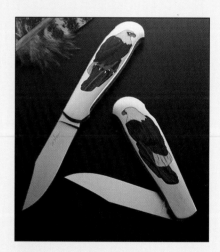

ABOVE
**Two views of "Eagle" folding knife by Harumi Hirayama.**

**The Ultimate in Basic Folders**
Ron Lake ● Steve Hoel ● Jess Horn ● Dick Hodgson ● Warren Osborne ● T. R. Overeynder ● Jim Corrado ● Durvyn Howard ● Dwight Towell ● W. D. Pease
**Marvelous Mechanisms**
Ray Appleton ● Michael Walker
**Dazzling Damascus**
James Schmidt ● Jerry Rados ● Barry Davis ● Stephen Schwarzer
**Embellished by the Makers**
Harumi Hirayama ● Michael and Patricia Walker ● H. H. Frank ● Shiro Furukawa ● Tim Herman ● Steve Jernigan ● Harvey McBurnette

RIGHT
**Three views of a Multalock folding push dagger by Ray Appleton. Titanium handle frame. Note how the complex release button retracts when the blade is in the closed position.**

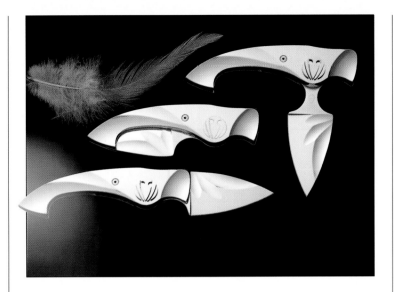

BELOW
**"Wings" folding dagger by Michael Walker. Total length when open 12 in (30.3cm). Fossilized walrus ivory handles. Titanium bolsters engraved and toned by Patricia Walker.**

sometimes other metals, from about a hundred to several thousand layers. When polished and etched, a damascus blade reveals its pattern – sometimes a simple watered effect, other times complex patterns or designs, including rippling American flags complete with thirteen stripes and fifty stars.

Exotic metals used for handles and fittings – gold, platinum, and iridium – enjoy a current vogue. Titanium, niobium, and even aluminium, can be toned to bright colours with heat, electricity, and chemicals. Michael and Patricia Walker pioneered this technique on folding knives, along with a much-improved version of the 1906 Cattaraugus "Liner Lock". They attracted a whole parade of imitators.

An up-and-coming fashion is a type of knife called "Gentlemen's knives", small yet exquisite and expensive hand-made folding knives. Most successful so far have been small jack knives with extra touches such as gold fittings. A few makers have tried pen knife and multi-blade designs, but many buyers are not ready to spend large sums on little knives, and most makers have not reached the pre-1940 Golden Age level of quality in small knives. I believe that these little gem-like knives will catch on, partly because of the growing popularity of folding knives and partly because of their close link to fine jewellery and watches.

A related area is true miniature knives; tiny, perfectly executed folding knives that are much too small to use. This market is well developed, with many active collectors.

# CHAPTER VII

# COUNTERFEITS

K nife counterfeiting for the purpose of cheating collectors began as a shady cottage industry in the 1950s, with the fabrication of fantasy bowie knives. I do not know exactly when fake pocketknives first appeared, but they were around in 1971 when I first got into the knife business. Like most beginners, I learned my first lessons about counterfeits the hard way, laying out good money for bad knives. I have never made the *same* mistake twice, but there are always new mistakes just waiting to be made.

As pocketknives have grown more popular and more valuable, fakes have grown more common. Most are still relatively easy for the experienced collector to spot, but beginners can be fooled by slick shiny fakes. Today at most knife shows there are entire tables offering nothing but fakes. Show sponsors have not yet come up with a satisfactory solution.

## WHERE IT WAS MADE
·············· CAN TELL YOU A LOT ··············

Most fake knives were not made in the same country as the originals which they attempt to copy, so their materials and construction are noticeably different from those of the genuine article. For example, most mass-produced fakes of older American knives are made in Germany and Japan, so once you

**ABOVE**
**Top: genuine Case XX 6249 "Copperhead" or "Viet Nam" pattern jack knife with red jigged bone handles. Bottom: counterfeit Case XX 6249.**

## NAZI POCKETKNIVES?

In the 1930s and 1940s the German Nazi party ordered millions upon millions of fancy dress daggers, decorated with party regalia, and in many patterns and variations. These daggers are now popular collector items (and widely faked).

One thing the Nazis did not order was fancy pocketknives. Yet at many knife shows, gun shows, or swap meets, one is sure to see what *look* like Nazi pocketknives. They have all the right regalia, sometimes even a portrait of Hitler or his "autograph". When one ex-Nazi official was shown one of these knives, he said, "We probably would have bought things like this back then, if someone had thought of them, but no one did."

These "Nazi" pocketknives are pure fantasies, dreamed up in the 1970s and sold to the swap-meet trade, mainly by Parker Cutlery Co of Tennessee. They have now been around long enough to start turning up at antiques stores and estate sales, but they are not genuine, and they have no value.

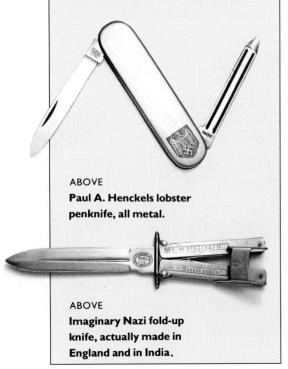

**ABOVE**
**Paul A. Henckels lobster penknife, all metal.**

**ABOVE**
**Imaginary Nazi fold-up knife, actually made in England and in India.**

learn to recognize German and Japanese craftsmanship – both usually good, but quite different from American style – these fakes will become obvious to you.

Long before there were knife collectors, there were already fakes – lots of them – littering the channels of cutlery commerce. In the 17th and 18th centuries Sheffield makers faked London brands. In the 19th century German cutlery firms made up English-sounding names to put on knives they sold in America, while in this century cutlers in India did the same thing.

Today Germans make fake American knives for American companies, Italians make fake German knives for German *and* American companies, and North Africans make fake Italian knives for their own consumption because they are cheaper than the real thing. Spaniards make fake French knives for local sale, and so, for that matter, do some French firms. The Japanese fake everyone's knives – and not on their own initiative, but because knife distributors in other countries ask them to (the Japanese are happy to oblige). Meanwhile Pakistani cutlers knock off the Japanese copies, the Chinese copy everyone, and everyone copies "Swiss Army" knives.

So what is a poor collector or other knife buyer to do? Look at knives, especially genuine knives, and study how they are made. Materials and workmanship are surer guides to where and when a knife was manufactured than the markings. Markings only matter when they are consistent with the rest of the knife.

### TYPES OF FAKERY

There are three basic types of fake knives. These are counterfeits, re-works, and fantasies.

- **COUNTERFEITS.** A counterfeit is a fake knife which was made in conscious imitation of an authentic knife. Most counterfeits are of decidedly inferior quality, compared to their originals, but beginners who have never seen an original first-hand are likely to be fooled by them. Experience is the best insurance against this type of fake. The overwhelming majority of knife collectors and dealers will be happy to loan you their experience and examine a knife that you are considering acquiring.

The threat of really high-quality counterfeits lurks just over the horizon, but so far it has not arrived (as far as I can tell). Anyone capable of making a counterfeit of, say, a Remington R1306

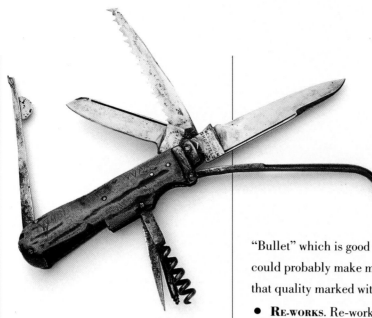

LEFT
**George Wostenholm, Sheffield, horseman's knife, genuine stag, repaired with an old Pennsylvania Knife Co blade; probably an old repair.**

"Bullet" which is good enough to fool an advanced collector, could probably make more money by making a folding knife of that quality marked with his own name.

- **RE-WORKS**. Re-works are a much more difficult category than counterfeits. A re-work is a genuine old knife that has been "improved" in some way. The improvement may be relatively minor, such as a patched handle crack or a tightened rivet.

The improvement may instead be a major one, such as an insignificant marking being ground away, to be replaced by a more popular brand. Most re-stamping is done with modern stamps and is easy for the experienced collector to spot since lettering styles have changed over the years. Some fakers have original old stamping dies, however, and then the collector must be familiar with a particular brand in order to avoid being fooled. Lazy fakers engrave or etch fake marks, which should not fool anyone – but they do.

A common form of re-working is the replacement of broken blades, springs, handle covers, or other components. There is a fine line between legitimate restoration, on one side, and fraud, on the other. A legitimate restoration usually incorporates correct original parts and is always revealed by the seller. Fraud is anything less.

- **FANTASY KNIVES**. Fantasy knives would be a glorious joke, if it were not that so many beginning collectors get caught out by them. A fantasy knife is one that a faker dreamed up and then marked with famous names in an effort to tie it to history. Fantasy knives are never based on real prototypes, so strictly speaking they are not counterfeits. Most are glaringly anachronistic in shape, materials, construction, or decoration, but the beginner may not realize this. Many fantasy knives would not function as knives, a sure clue that a "knife" is not genuine.

## IT'S IN PRINT, SO IT MUST BE TRUE

I once met a collector, an educated professional, who did not believe in counterfeits. For example, if a knife said WINCHESTER on it, as far as he was concerned it was a Winchester knife. He knew perfectly well that some of the knives that he owned marked WINCHESTER had been made by the Winchester Repeating Arms Company in Connecticut in the 1920s and 1930s, while others were made in Germany in the 1970s, in Japan in the 1980s, in Pennsylvania in the 1990s, or in somebody's basement last week.

None of this bothered him. The knives all said WINCHESTER, so to him they were all WINCHESTER knives, and to him they were all equally valuable.

There, of course, lay the problem. No doubt a few other people share this gentleman's innocent outlook, but most do not. If he ever wants to sell his knives, the ones really made by Winchester will sell right away, while most of the rest will not sell at all.

# VIII
CHAPTER

# KEYS TO COLLECTING
# POCKETKNIVES

ABOVE
**O. Barnett Tool Co,
Newark, NJ, HHH plier
knife, bone stag handles.**

The simplest approach to pocketknife collecting can be stated in two sentences: 1) Collect whatever you like. 2) They're your knives, so do whatever you wish to them.

This system will work perfectly in either of two circumstances: 1) If you live on a desert island where you will never meet another collector. 2) If you are so fabulously wealthy that you will never need to sell or trade any of your knives.

I actually know knife collectors in both of these situations, but the chances are that neither of them applies to you. Therefore it will behoove you to pay attention to what other collectors want and expect.

·························· FASHION ··························

As we have seen, there are lots of different types and brands of pocketknives which can be collected. At any given time, some of these will be fashionable among large numbers of collectors, while others will not. Fashions are more changeable in modern hand-made knives than they are in antique pocketknives, but the fashions in both do change significantly.

All it takes to start a fashion is two aggressive and free-

**TOP ROW**
**(Left to right): recent Schrade barlow knife, smooth bone handles; Parker Cutlery Co miniature jack knife, abalone shell handles; 1980s Case light trapper, red jigged bone handles.**

**MIDDLE**
**Late 19th century large Sheffield horseman's multi-blade with stag handles, made for A.G. Alford Sporting Goods Co, Baltimore, Md.**

**BOTTOM ROW**
**(Left to right): Ka-Bar jack knife with razor and spey blades, wood handles; Case serpentine jack, genuine stag handles; Parker Cutlery Co small lockback, pearl handles.**

spending collectors competing for the same type of knives. If their rivalry persists for any length of time, other people will join in and that particular market niche will take on a life of its own. Sometimes the enthusiasm will survive the departure of its original founders; other times it will not.

·················· CONDITION ··················

A close second in significance to fashion among collectors is the question of condition. In pocketknife collecting, condition is at least as important as it is in coin collecting – probably even more so. A knife in excellent *unsharpened* condition is worth significantly more than a knife in lesser condition, and knowledgeable advanced collectors will not buy knives in lesser condition at any price. If you clean or sharpen a knife to "improve" its appearance, you are destroying most of its resale value.

Many collectors will only consider knives in "mint" condition. This means knives that were never used, never carried, and certainly never cleaned or sharpened. Modern knives, including hand-made, limited editions and standard factory types, as a rule

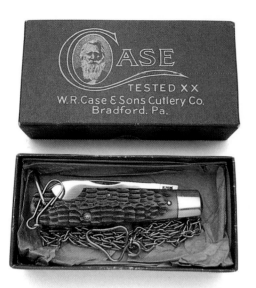

ABOVE
**Case Tested XX easy-open barehead standard jack with shackle and chain, jigged bone handles, original box.**

LEFT
**NKCA (National Knife Collectors Association) 1992 Club Knife, trapper pattern made by Queen Cutlery Co.**

are only collectible in mint condition. A used modern knife still has value as a knife to use, but that is all.

Mint condition antique pocketknives are a delicate topic, precisely because their condition is so delicate. Their materials are inherently unstable: blades and springs rust; fittings discolour; handle materials shrink or crack. Some long-time collectors shy away from mint knives, because one day of extreme humidity could wipe out their investment. Despite this, there is now, and likely will remain, a strong market for old knives that are truly in mint condition.

················ CLEANING ················

The rules of cleaning are simple: 1) When in doubt, don't. 2) When not in doubt, *definitely* don't.

There are two reasons for these rules. 1) Over-enthusiastic cleaning will destroy whatever remains of a knife's original finish, substantially reducing its value. 2) A cautious buyer must assume that a heavily cleaned knife has been re-worked, even if it has not. Cautious buyers do not buy knives which they suspect are re-works.

As with all rules, there are a few exceptions. For example, do gently wipe off fingerprints with a clean soft cloth. Do apply one drop of light machine oil or Japanese sword oil to the joint of each blade (*do not ever* use lubricants containing solvents or dryers, such as 3-in-1 Oil or WD-40). Do clean lint and grease out of handles with a wooden toothpick. Do remove spots of active (red) rust with oil and a sharp needle. However, if you care at all about the aesthetic, historical, or monetary value of a knife, do not do anything else to it.

················ STORAGE ················

This is a difficult question, not yet satisfactorily resolved, even by the major museums. The goals are fairly straightforward: stable temperature, stable humidity, acid-free containers and atmosphere, protection from Dermestid carpet beetles (whose tiny larvae devour horn and other organic materials). Acid-free paper and cardboard are sold by picture framers; acid-free boxes by museum supply firms.

Rooms where knives are stored *must* be climate controlled, for both temperature and humidity. Bank vaults are usually safe if the bank itself is air-conditioned.

Some collectors store knives in open boxes or wrapped up in protective "tarnish-proof" cloth. I have seen both methods work, and I have seen both methods fail dismally. Museums favour open boxes (acid-free, of course), but I have seen boxed knives rust away to shapeless brown lumps.

Never store knives inside leather sheaths or purses. Many de luxe old pocketknives came with elegant clasp-top or snap-flap knife purses; preserve these, but not with the knife inside. Check your knives frequently, and arrest any deterioration that you notice.

···················· LEARNING ····················

The more you learn about knives, the happier you will be, even if you decide never to collect them. Right now you are doing the second-best thing to learn about knives: reading about them. If you want to read more, a bibliography follows.

The best way to learn about knives is to go to knife shows, knife shops, and museums where you can look at and study lots of knives. All knives can teach you something useful or interesting, even the knives in your kitchen drawer.

Every knife fancier should try to visit the Sheffield City Museum in Britain; the Solingen Blade Museum in Germany; the National Knife Museum, in Chattanooga, Tennessee; and the American Military Edged Weaponry Museum in Intercourse, Pennsylvania. Other museums, such as the Smithsonian's National Museum of American History in Washington, and the Victoria & Albert Museum in London, have important knife collections, but these are usually not on display, and prior arrangements must be made to view them.

At knife shows and in shops, remember a few basic rules of courtesy. 1) Do not handle knives without permission. 2) Never touch the blade or the edge of any knife offered or displayed as a collector's item. 3) Never open more than one blade of an antique folding knife at a time.

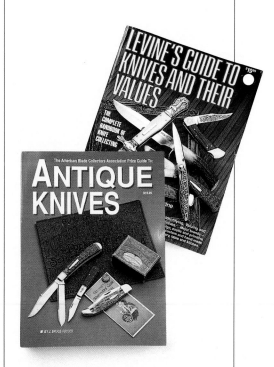

ABOVE
**Reading is a good way to further your knowledge of pocketknives. Pictured here are *Levine's Guide*, 1985 edition (the 3rd edition was published in 1993), and J. Bruce Voyle's *Antique Knives* (see Further Reading).**

# FURTHER READING ABOUT
# POCKETKNIVES

········· KNIFE MAGAZINES ·········

## EUROPE

### La Passion des Couteaux

Editions Phenix, 25 rue Mademoiselle, 75015 Paris,
France

In French. Covers knives around the world, with
emphasis on France, USA, Germany; custom knives,
factory knives, good historical coverage. On newsstands
in French-speaking countries. There was briefly an
English language edition.

## AFRICA

### African Blade

PO Box 5564, Cape Town 8000, Republic of South
Africa

## ASIA

### Knife

World Photo Press, 3rd Floor, Daisan Koushin Bldg,
2–3–16 Kabuki-Cho, Shinjuku-Ku, Tokyo T160,
Japan

In Japanese. Highest-quality production of all knife
magazines. Extensive coverage of hand-made knives
from USA and Japan, factory knives from around the
world; technical and how-to articles, knife show
coverage in colour, some historical coverage. Most
issues feature my "From USA Report". On newsstands
in Japan.

## US

### National Knife Magazine

National Knife Collectors Association (NKCA)
PO Box 21070, Chattanooga TN 37421, USA

Official magazine of the NKCA (which runs the National
Knife Museum). Focus on old pocketknives, limited
editions; also custom knives, military knives. Includes
my "Knife Lore" column, frequent features by Simon
Moore of England on ancient and medieval knives, John
Goins on mystery knives, Butch Winter on custom
knives, show calendar. Free sample copy on request.

### Blade Magazine, Edges, Blade Trade

Blade Publications, PO Box 22007, Chattanooga
TN 37422, USA

*Blade* is the largest-circulation knife magazine, and is
available on US and some European newsstands, and in
many cutlery shops. Features hand-made knives, knife
shows, Knifemakers Guild news, bowies, books, lots of
advertisements. *Edges* features antique pocketknives,
military knives, limited editions; lots of up-to-date
prices. *Blade Trade* is for cutlery retailers.

### Knife World

Knife World Publications, PO Box 3395, Knoxville
TN 37927, USA

Tabloid format. Features my "Whut Izzit" column
identifying and valuing unusual knives for readers; also
old pocketknives, hand-made knives, history,
interviews, listing of local knife clubs, knife show
calendar; offers very large selection of knife books for
sale by mail worldwide. Free sample copy on request.

### Knives Illustrated

McMullen Publishing, Inc, 2145 West La Palma Ave,
Anaheim CA 92801–1785, USA

Focus on hand-made knives; also detailed, well-
illustrated articles for the do-it-yourself knifemaker.

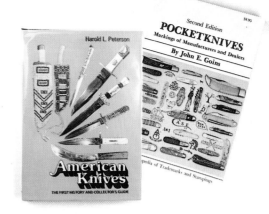

**Fighting Knives**
LFP Inc, 9171 Wilshire Blvd Suite 300, Beverly
Hills CA 90210, USA
Field and combat knives, factory and hand-made;
includes reviews, maker profiles, some history.

**Sporting Blades**
15875–F SE 114th St, Clackamas OR 97015, USA
Tabloid format. Contemporary sport and combat knives,
factory and hand-made.

## ········ US KNIFE ANNUALS ··········

**Knives '93** (13th Annual) etc
DBI Books, 4092 Commercial Avenue, Northbrook
IL 60062, USA
Book format. THE knife directory since 1981. Includes
detailed worldwide listings, plus solid feature articles
and hundreds of photographs. Indispensable. Through
Arms & Armour Press, London, in Europe, Africa and
Asia; through Lothian Books in Australia.

**Gutmann Knives**
Aqua-Field Publishing Co, Inc, 66 West Gilbert
Street, Shrewsbury NJ 07702, USA
Magazine format. Focus on knives distributed by
Gutmann Cutlery, Inc; also includes history, technical,
and how-to articles.

## DISCONTINUED CUTLERY ············ MAGAZINES ················

*Messer und Feile* (in German), published 1894–1912.
*American Cutler*, also *Cutlery Journal*, and *Paine's
Cutlery Journal*, published 1909–1940s, sometimes as
separate magazines, sometimes combined.
*International Cutler*, published in England 1951–1953.
*Blue Mill Blade*, published *circa* 1972–1977 (forerunner
of the *National Knife Magazine*).

## ·············· KNIFE BOOKS ··············

### GENERAL

**Levine, Bernard.** *Levine's Guide to Knives and Their
Values*. Northbrook, Illinois: DBI Books, 1993. The
standard introduction and reference on all types of
knives: folding and fixed blade, old and new, factory and
hand-made. Distributed in Europe, Africa and Asia
through Arms & Armour Press and through Lothian
Books in Australia.

**Moore, Simon.** *Pen Knives and Other Folding Knives.*
Aylesbury, UK: Shire Publications, 1988. A brief but
excellent primer by the most scholarly writer in the field.
**Peterson, Harold.** *American Knives.* New York City:
Scribners, 1958. The first, and for many years the best,
general book on the subject. Though somewhat dated, it
is still worthwhile.
**Weyer, Jim.** *Knives, Points of Interest.* III vols. Toledo,
Ohio: Weyer International, 1990. Colour photographs of
fine hand-made knives.

### ENCYCLOPAEDIAS

**Goins, John.** *Encyclopedia of Cutlery Markings.*
Knoxville, Tennessee: Knife World Publications, 1986.
Thousands of brand names, with dates and history
of most.
**Mayes, Robert.** *Knife Album.* Privately printed, 1970.
A large hardbound volume of old catalogue reprints.
**Pankiewicz, Philip.** *New England Cutlery.* Gilman,
Connecticut: Hollytree Publications, 1986. "Scrapbook"
of history and documentation on dozens of
manufacturers in Connecticut, Massachusetts, Rhode
Island, Maine, New Hampshire, and Vermont.

### POCKETKNIFE PRICE GUIDES

**Levine, Bernard.** *Levine's Guide to Knives and Their
Values.* Northbrook, Illinois: DBI Books, 1993. *See*
General listing.
**Price, C. Houston.** *The Official Price Guide, Collector
Knives.* 10th ed. New York City: House of Collectibles,
1991. Fairly detailed coverage of popular brands,
selectively illustrated (8 pages in colour).
**Russell, A. G.** *A. G. Russell's Knife Trader's Guide.*
Cut'n Shoot, Texas: Paul Wahl Corporation, 1991.
Actual prices realized by the leading consignment knife
dealer in the world; mainly hand-made knives. Pocket
size. No illustrations.

**Sargent, Jim.** *American Premium Guide to Knives and Razors.* 3rd ed. Florence, Alabama: Books Americana, 1992. Extremely detailed coverage of eight popular brands: Case, Remington, Pal, Browning, Keen Kutter, Western States, Queen and Winchester; mainly illustrated with photographs (12 pages in colour).

**Stewart, Ron & Ritchie, Roy.** *The Standard Knife Collector's Guide.* Paducah, Kentucky: Collector Books, 1986. Innovative pricing approach, along with a lot of useful information.

**Voyles, J. Bruce.** *American Blade Collectors Association Price Guide to Antique Knives.* Chattanooga, Tennessee: American Blade, 1990. Includes moderately detailed coverage of 31 brands, illustrated with old catalogue cuts; limited coverage of other brands; useful background material and charts.

## SPECIAL TOPICS

**Benson, Ragnar.** *Switchblade, The Ace of Blades.* Boulder, Colorado: Paladin Press, 1990.

**Brewster, Mel.** *Remington Bullet Knives.* 2d ed. Tacoma, Washington: Collector Knives Press, 1991. Detailed study of all known variants, plus reissues, posters and related knives.

**Cole, M. H.** *U.S. Military Knives, Bayonets, and Machetes, Books III and IV.* Birmingham, Alabama: privately printed, 1990. Detailed extensive coverage, mainly using superb line drawings, of both standard and unusual military knives.

**Domenech, Abel A.** *Del Facón al Bowie.* Buenos Aires, Argentina: Ediciones El Alamo, 1988. Mainly about gaucho knives and bowies, but has one chapter on "Cuchillos de bolsillo y plegables (cortaplumas y navajas)". In Spanish.

**Giles, James S.** *Case, The First 100 Years.* Sevierville, Tenessee: Smoky Mountain Knife Works, 1989. Handsomely produced volume, lots of early photographs and illustrations, plus colour plates of the factory knife collection.

**Jenkins, Clare & McClarence, Stephen.** *On the Knife Edge, the Inside Story of the Sheffield Cutlery Industry.* Sheffield, UK. Sheffield City Libraries, 1989. Interviews with surviving old-time craftsmen and women.

**Johnson, Thomas.** *Collecting the Edged Weapons of the Third Reich.* 6 volumes, with more planned. Fredericksburg, Virginia: Johnson Reference Books, 1992. Thorough, detailed, accurate, clearly written, well illustrated.

**Karsten, Bill.** *Silver Folding Fruit Knives.* Knoxville, Tennessee: Knife World Publications, 1986. Excellent monograph by a leading collector.

**Levine, Bernard.** *The Knife Collection of Albert Blevins.* Grafton, Vermont: Allon Schoerner Associates, 1988. Background and inventory of a very valuable collection of hand-made knives, including the three dozen now in the Smithsonian's National Museum of American History. Colour photographs.

**Ristinen, Lester.** *The Knives of Finland.* Wolf Lake, Minnesota: Suomi Shop, 1990.

**Silvey, Michael & Boyd, Gary.** *United States Military Knives, Collector's Guide.* Sacramento, California: privately printed, 1989. Not as thorough as Cole (*see* above), but illustrated with photographs.

**Swayne, Allen P.** *The Case Knife Story.* Knoxville, Tennessee: Knife World Publications, 1987. Illustrates and dates over 75 Case blade stampings.

**Tweedale, Geoffrey.** *Giants of Sheffield Steel.* Sheffield, UK: Sheffield City Libraries, 1986. Biographies of ten key figures.

————. *Sheffield Steel and America. A Century of Commercial and Technological Interdependence.* Cambridge, UK: Cambridge University Press, 1987. Scholarly history.

## TECHNIQUE BOOKS

**Kelley, Ben, Jr.** *The Complete Book of Pocketknife Repair.* Chattanooga, Tennessee: American Blade, 1982. Methods of one of the last Case factory authorized repairmen.

**Lake, Ron, Centofante, Frank & Clay, Wayne.** *How to Make Folding Knives.* Chattanooga, Tennessee: American Blade, 1988. Techniques of top hand makers.

## ··· OUT-OF-PRINT KNIFE BOOKS ···
(A selection of useful titles to look for)

Original hardware and cutlery catalogues: priceless primary sources.

Cutlery catalogue reprints. Dozens of old pocketknife catalogues have been reprinted since 1970, all but two or three are now out of print. All are both useful and interesting.

**Adams, Bill, Voyles, Bruce & Moss, Terry.** *The Antique Bowie Knife Book.* 1990. Dazzling huge full-colour book, includes 14 big Sheffield folding bowie knives.

**Bardy, Ed.** *Advertising with a Sharp Edge.* 1st ed. 1972; 2nd ed. 1975. Advertising and figural knives, lots of photographs, historical background.

**Baronti, Giancarlo.** *Coltelli D'Italia.* 1986. Italian pocketknives, and tales of their criminal associations. All-colour, handsome book. In Italian.

**Bates, John & Schippers, James.** *The Custom Knife II, The Book of Pocket Knives and Folding Hunters.* 1974. A pioneer work about pioneering makers.

**Bement, Lewis D.** *The Cutlery Story.* 1950. Excellent primer by the president of Russell-Harrington.

**de Bondaroy, Fougeroux.** *L'Art du Coutelier en Ouvrages Communs.* 1771. Factory mass-production of pocketknives more than two centuries ago. Handsomely illustrated. Companion volume to Perret. In French.

**Buster, Frank.** *The International Fight'n Rooster Knife Collector, 1977 thru 1983.* 1984. Photographs and photocopies of the first seven years of this popular limited-production pocketknife brand, plus photographs inside the workshop in Solingen where the knives are made.

**Cassidy, William.** *Knife Digest.* 1st ed. 1974, 2nd ed. 1976. Full of interesting knife lore.

**Collins, Blackie.** *The Pocketknife Manual.* 1976. How to make and repair, by a leading knife designer. Includes a 40-page interview with Felix Mirando, co-founder of Imperial, illustrated with factory method photographs.

**Cowgill, J. et al.** *Knives and Scabbards.* Medieval Finds, 1987.

**Dyson, B. Ronald.** *A Glossary of Words and Dialect Formerly Used in the Sheffield Trades.* 1936, reprinted 1979. Fascinating.

**Ehrhardt, Roy.** *The Encyclopedia of Old Pocketknives.* Catalog reprints, mainly Maher & Grosh, an old retail firm in Toledo, Ohio.

**Ferguson, Lavona & Dewey.** *The Romance of Knife Collecting.* 4th ed. 1976. A ground-breaking work, histories of many popular pocketknife brands. Still useful, if dated.

————. *The Romance of Collecting Case Knives.* 4th (pink) ed. 1978. Others have covered Case knives more recently, but this is still a useful book.

————. *The Romance of Collecting Cattaraugus, Robeson, Russell, and Queen Knives.* 1978. Catalogue reprints, history, and more.

**Forton, Rafael Martinez Del Peral.** *Las Navajas, Un Estudio y Coleccion.* Spanish clasp knives. I have never seen a copy, but I would like to. In Spanish.

**Frazier, Charles & Ferguson, Revis.** *The Knife Collectors Handbook.* Catalogue reprints, thumbnail histories, well printed, useful.

**Himsworth, J. B.** *The Story of Cutlery.* 1953. A classic.

**Hollis, Durwood.** *Petersen's Complete Book of Knives.* 1988.

**Landrin, M. H.** *Manuel du Coutelier.* 1835. An early pocket-sized, how-to book. In French.

**Leader, Robert Eaton.** *History of the Company of Cutlers in Hallamshire in the County of York.* 2 vols., 1905. Official history of the Sheffield Cutlers' Guild. *See* Peach, L. du G., for continuation.

**Levine, Bernard.** *Knifemakers of Old San Francisco.* 1978.

————. *The Knife Identification and Value Guide.* 1981. The first three years of my "Whut Izzit" column from *Knife World.*

**Lewis, Jack & Hughes, B. R.** *The Gun Digest Book of Folding Knives.* 1977. Visits to knife factories and knifemaker shops, a good snapshot of that time.

**Lloyd, G. I. H.** *The Cutlery Trades.* 1913 (also later reprints). A classic on Sheffield methods.

**Merriam, R. et al.** *The History of the John Russell Cutlery Company.* 1976. This started as a school project and became a handsome professional-quality book.

**Myers, Ben & Lowell.** *An Introduction to Switchblade Knives.* 1982. History, mechanical principles, price guide, and photographs, including some in colour.

**Nielsen, James R.** *Knives and the Law.* 1980. A brief annotated work on the language and provisions of various US knife laws.

**Pagé, Camille.** *La Coutellerie Depuis L'origine Jusqu'à Nos Jours.* VI vols., 1896–1902. Superb worldwide coverage by a leading cutlery manufacturer, collector, and historian of the time. Includes reprint of some of J. Perret's plates, plus hundreds of original ones. (Also *see* Victorinox below.) In French.

**Parker, James & Voyles, Bruce.** *The Rodgers Exhibition and Ceremonial Knives, and Other Fine Selected Cutlery Items.* Elegant full-colour catalogue, includes photographs reproduced from Rodgers's *Under Five Sovereigns.*

—————. *Official Price Guide to Collector Knives.* 1st–9th eds, 1976–1987. Current edition is by Houston Price (see above).

**Peach, L. du G.** *The Company of Cutlers in Hallamshire in the County of York, 1906–1956.* 1960. Continuation of R. E. Leader.

**Perret, Jean-Jacques.** *L'Art du Coutelier.* III vols. 1771. Still the best knifemaking how-to ever published. Incredible folio-sized plates. Perret said that the real test of a master cutler was to be able to draw a steel rod into a wire 6 inches (15 cm) long and ⅙ inch (0.4 cm) in diameter and then, using a breast drill, to make a 1/12-inch (0.2 cm) diameter hole through it – the long way. Volumes II and III are about surgical instruments. In French.

—————. *La Vie de la Coutellerie.* His autobiography. In French.

**Platts, Harvey.** *The Knife Makers Who Went West.* 1978. History of Western States Cutlery Co, also of Platts and Case, by the then-president and son of the founder. Superbly illustrated including reprints of all catalogues to that date.

**Price, C. Houston (ed.).** *The Best of Knife World.* 1st ed 1980, 2nd ed 1983 (3rd ed in press). Selected features from the popular periodical.

**de Riaz, Yvan.** *The Book of Knives.* 1978. Good introduction with fine photographs, many in colour. English, French, Spanish, and probably other language editions.

**Joseph Rodgers and Sons.** *Under Five Sovereigns.* 1918. Official company history.

**Sargent, Jim & Schleyer, Jim.** *Case Factory Endorsed Pocket Price Guide.* 3rd ed 1985. Detailed and portable. Largely superseded by Sargent's *American Premium Guide . . .* (*see* above), but the listing of Case

contract "specials" and limited editions (pp 157–179) is unique.

**Schreier, Konrad, F. Jr.** *Marble's Knives and Axes.* 1978. The Marble's Safety Hunting Knife, made in nearly a score of variants from 1902 to 1942, is much in demand among collectors.

**Smith, Joseph.** *Explanation or Key to the Various Manufactures of Sheffield.* 1816 (reprinted 1975). The very first illustrated catalogue of cutlery and tools made for the US market. Wonderful pictures of wonderful knives. Some reproduced in *Levine's Guide.*

**Stidham, Rhett.** *Napanoch. "A White Man's Knife with a Red Man's Name".* 1972. Brief history of this firm which became the nucleus of Winchester's cutlery operation, plus catalogue reprint and splendid old factory interior photographs.

**Taber, Martha Van Hoesen.** *A History of the Cutlery Industry in the Connecticut Valley.* 1955. Her PhD dissertation; it is scholarly, readable, and a basic reference. No illustrations.

**Tudor, Tracy.** *The Old Knife Book.* A good and varied selection of catalogue reprints, well printed.

**Victorinox.** *The Knife and its History.* 1984. Victorinox, Switzerland, centennial volume, includes reproductions of many plates from C. Pagé, old Elsener catalogue pages, colour photos inside factory (editions in many languages).

**Walter, John.** *Sword and Bayonet Makers of Imperial Germany.* 1973. A small encyclopaedia of German cutlery firms. Very useful.

**Warner, Ken.** *Knives '81 – Knives '92. See* description under US Knife Annuals.

**Washer, Richard.** *Sheffield Bowie and Pocket-knife Makers.* 1974. A small encyclopaedia. Interesting but inaccurate.

**Welch, Charles.** *History of the Cutlers' Company of London.* II vols, 1923.

**Whitham, J. H. & Vickers, D.** *Register of Trademarks of the Cutlers' Company of Sheffield.* 1919.

**Whitham, J. H. & Sykes, A.** *Register of Trademarks of the Cutlers' Company of Sheffield.* 1953.

**Williamson, William.** *I*XL means I Excel.* 1973. A brief history of G. Wostenholm & Sons.

**Woods, Jim.** *Guns and Ammo Guidebook to Knives and Edged Weapons.* 1974. A slim but superbly useful volume.

**George Wostenholm & Sons.** *The House of Wostenholm 1745–1945.* 1945. Official company history.

## NATIONAL AND INTERNATIONAL KNIFE COLLECTOR ORGANIZATIONS

**National Knife Collectors Association**
(NKCA)
PO Box 21070
Chattanooga
Tennessee 37421
USA
Publishes NATIONAL KNIFE MAGAZINE (free sample copy on request), and operates the National Knife Museum, 7201 Shallowford Rd, Chattanooga, Tennessee 37421, USA

There are more than 50 non-profit state and regional knife-collector clubs in the United States. Many of them sponsor knife shows and swap-meets, most of them offer annual limited edition club knives, and all of them welcome overseas members to join by mail. For an up-to-date list of knife clubs, knife shows, and knife books for sale by mail, write for a FREE sample copy of KNIFE WORLD magazine: KW Publications, PO Box 3395, Knoxville, Tennessee 37917, USA.

**Canadian Knife Collectors Club**
Route 1
Milton
Ontario L9T 2X5
Canada

**Knifemakers Guild**
PO Box 928
Madisonville
Tennessee 37354
USA
A collector may become an Honorary Member for US$10 per year.

## FOR-PROFIT KNIFE CLUBS

**Knife Collectors Club Inc**
1705 Hiway 71 N
Springdale
Arkansas 72764
USA

**Australasian Knife Collectors**
PO Box 268
Morley WA 6062
Australia

**American Blade Collectors Association**
PO Box 22007
Chattanooga
Tennessee 37422
USA

## MUSEUMS WITH IMPORTANT KNIFE COLLECTIONS

**Note:** In all but the specialized knife museums, the knives are generally not on public display. Prior arrangements must be made to view the collections in storage.

**Sheffield City Museums**
Sheffield
England

**Victoria and Albert Museum**
London
England

**German Blade Museum**
Solingen
Germany

**Solingen Industry Museum**
Solingen
Germany

**Maison des Couteliers**
Thiers
France

**Log Cabin Museum**
Seki City
Japan

**National Knife Museum**
Chattanooga
Tennessee, USA

**American Military Edged Weaponry Museum**
Intercourse
Pennsylvania, USA

**Smithsonian Institution**
National Museum of American History
Washington, DC, USA

**Metropolitan Museum of Art**
New York, New York, USA

**California Academy of Sciences**
San Francisco
California, USA

**The Oakland Museum**
Oakland
California, USA

**Randall Made Knives**
Orlando
Florida, USA

**National Metal Museum**
Memphis
Tennessee, USA

**Essex Institute**
Salem
Massachusetts, USA

**Museum of the Fur Trade**
Chadron
Nebraska, USA

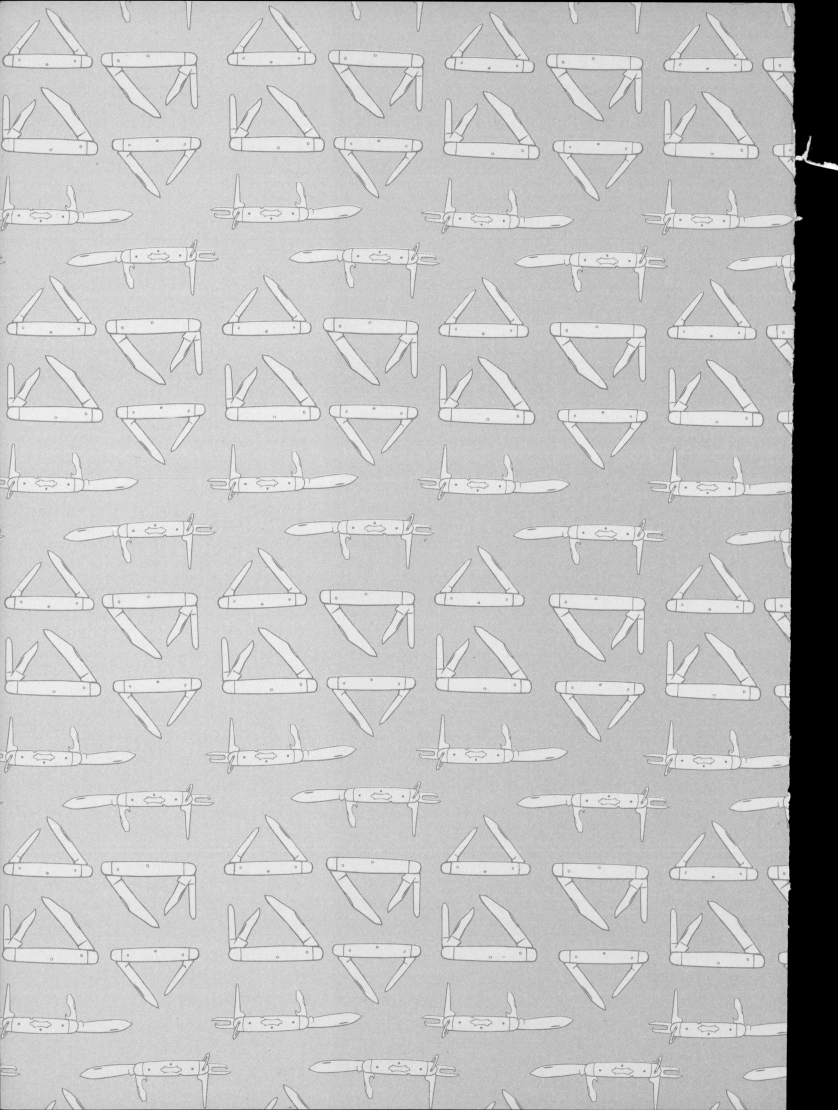